GARDENING
with
children

GARDENING
with
children

Beth Richardson
Photographs by Lynn Karlin

The Taunton Press

Taunton
BOOKS & VIDEOS

for fellow enthusiasts

Cover photo: Lynn Karlin

Text © 1998 by Beth Richardson
Photographs © 1998 by Lynn Karlin, except where noted
Photographs on pages 10 (left), 21, 32, 37, 53, and 54 © 1998 by The Taunton Press, Inc.
Illustrations © 1998 by The Taunton Press, Inc.
All rights reserved.

Printed in the United States of America
10 9 8 7 6 5 4 3 2

The Taunton Press, Inc.
63 South Main Street
PO Box 5506
Newtown, CT 06470-5506
e-mail: tp@taunton.com

Distributed by Publishers Group West

Library of Congress Cataloging-in-Publication Data
Richardson, Beth.
      Gardening with children / Beth Richardson; photographs by Lynn Karlin.
           p.   cm.
      Includes index.
      ISBN 1-56158-192-5
      1. Children's gardens. I. Title
      SB457.R484   1998
      635'.083—dc21   97-32697
                                                              CIP

To my sons, Bennett and Seth, who never fail to bring joy to my life.

To my husband, Peter, whose love, devout loyalty, frequent pep talks, and willingness to have gardening tools, photography equipment, and unfamiliar children scattered throughout our home provided me with the energy to write this book. Having you by my side made it all possible.

Acknowledgments

Gardening with Children was a labor of love, requiring dedication from many more people than me.

My family, including our poodle, Cyrus, and lovebird, Oscar, endured hours of affection deprivation, as well as excess attention from children they had never before met. Most of all, the children and parents involved in the photographing of this book, who participated out of interest, friendship, and curiosity, showed a commitment that I will treasure for years to come.

Special thanks to the Peck-Lishness family, who willingly starred in pictures, often at a moment's notice and at odd hours of the morning to catch the gentle light of sunrise. I cherish their friendship. Thanks also to the Bond, Cantara, Gibson, Grotton, Kline, Schoppee, Talbert, VanWormer, Walsh, Weinstein, and Weschler families for dressing their children in bright colors and enthusiastically embracing this project as their own.

And, finally, to Lynn Karlin, the gifted photographer who brought the text to life. Her patience and tolerance with 5-year-olds who refused to smile and 14-year-olds who challenged her professional credentials were truly amazing. Most amazing, though, is her skill with the camera—it is a gift to us all.

Contents

INTRODUCTION   2

SECTION 1   Including Children in Daily Gardening Activity

CHAPTER ONE   What to Plant   6

CHAPTER TWO   Laying Out the Garden   18

CHAPTER THREE   Building the Garden   32

CHAPTER FOUR   Preparing the Soil Organically   42

CHAPTER FIVE   Planting the Garden   63

CHAPTER SIX   Tending the Garden   83

SECTION 2   Making Gardening Fun for Children

CHAPTER SEVEN   Theme Gardens   110

CHAPTER EIGHT   Family Garden Projects   129

USDA PLANT HARDINESS ZONE MAP   150

RESOURCES   151

INDEX   152

Introduction

Until just a couple of years ago, I had never even thought of combining gardening and parenting. Gardening was all mine, one of the few things—unlike my breakfast, jewelry, clothes, lunch, home, car, and dinner—that I simply didn't want to be drooled on, painted in primary colors, or taken into the bathtub. The same is true for many other parents who like to garden.

Gardening is a time for quiet and calm, order and beauty—an opportunity for personal reflection and creativity. Parenting, on the other hand, particularly of small children, is often a time for chaos and noise. How, therefore, can you thin out a row of arugula or contemplate a fresh tomato-and-basil salad while a 3-year-old rips the cover off a sippy cup and pours the juice down your back? Many parents often decide they can't do both. Given the fact that the children are a permanent part of their lives, a garden regrettably gets the heave-ho.

But even though I am the mother of two *very* rambunctious boys who require a lot of my time and attention, I love gardening too much to give it up. So one summer, I decided to make parenting and gardening work simultaneously. I wanted to create a fabulous family garden, hoping my children would view gardening as a wondrous adventure and the garden as a playground and laboratory. I wanted my children to work and dream and feel accomplished, to learn the delicate balance of nature, to gather an appreciation for sustenance, and at the same time, to have some pure and simple fun. I wanted my children to feel that their gardening activities were the heart of the garden's beauty, without feeling overwhelmed and responsible for the whole garden. I wanted, quite simply, a satisfying balance for all.

With these things in mind, I began looking in books for ideas on child-centered gardening activities to include in a family garden. I wanted to integrate my children into the garden, not abdicate the garden to them. Unfortunately, the only information I found was how to create a child-centered garden that depended on an adult—abdication, not integration. This book was borne out of my desire to give other parent-gardeners like me information on how to create an adult-centered garden that included and celebrated children.

Just as I thrive to create beautiful gardens that will delight my children, I have tried to create a fascinating and enjoyable book for adults that will help them introduce children to the delights of gardening. I read gardening books and cookbooks like others read captivating novels. I devour them, become part of the experiences they describe, taste the complex flavors, and smell the fresh herbs while turning the pages. In this book, I have tried to offer you the very same experience, though you may smell peanut butter and jelly mixed in with the fresh basil.

But don't expect a lot of "kid speak" here. This is most certainly a book for adults. You will find no large block letters or recitations of the gardening alphabet. What you will find are delightful photographs, intricate plans, honest conversation, and information aimed at including the children in your life in the gardens of your life—all in a way that will satisfy your need for contemplative time in the garden and nurturing time with the children that you so love.

Including Children in Daily Gardening Activity

Gardening is enjoyed by adults because of the sense of creation we gather from bringing something from the garden to the dinner table. But gardening can also be an incredibly powerful experience for children. Just imagine the look of wonder on your children's faces as they discover new abilities or skills or finally understand a concept that previously escaped their comprehension.

No matter what their ages—whether first graders or middle schoolers—children can find a place in the garden. In this section, I'll explain how to include your children in daily gardening activities—from planning and building to planting and tending. I do not suggest that you hand your garden over to your children, but rather that you teach them about gardening in ways that are satisfying for you and fun for them.

By doing so, you and your children will work and play together and will experience firsthand the beauty and complexity of the garden cycle. You will have fabulous produce to eat all summer long and will get to experiment in the garden with varieties you may have thought you would never see until the children were well ensconced in a college cafeteria, miles away.

CHAPTER ONE

What to Plant

A colorful seed catalog is an ideal way to introduce your children to the idea of a family garden.

The first important decision that any gardener must make is what to plant. But the plant choices take on even more importance when you are planning a family garden and including your children in the whole process rather than just in the eating part. Let's face it. If your children don't like what is planted, they won't be interested, and worst of all, they won't eat the result of your efforts. You, therefore, could be stuck with bushels of vegetables that will become very old, very fast.

With any garden you plan, the first step is typically to make a plant list. When planning a garden in which children will be involved, you have to choose plants that will do well in your climate, that mature quickly, and that are family favorites. In this chapter, I'll show how you can begin to get your children involved in choosing plants for the garden, and I'll also tell you about a few plants that are perfect for small hands, curious eyes, and finicky tastes. When you gather the family together to work on the plant list, begin by explaining to the children how climate affects plant growth, as this may limit their choices.

How Your Climate Affects Plant Choices

If you are an experienced gardener, you are more than likely familiar with the weather conditions in your area and understand how they affect your plants and soil. Your children, however, may not be familiar with these concepts. It is your job to introduce them to this information so that they understand why your garden may or may not support certain vegetables or fruits.

The U.S. Department of Agriculture (USDA) has divided North America into planting regions, which are called hardiness zones. These hardiness zones indicate a range of the average minimum temperatures in a given area. Researchers and hybridizers test plants and then assign hardiness designations to them.

Your best resources for plants that will do well in your climate are seed catalogs that originate from your state or a similar climate. These climate-specific catalogs provide parents with a kind of automatic safety valve in that most of them will not sell seeds that will not produce in their climate.

If you can't find a climate-specific catalog, simply choose a catalog from a reputable seed company. A good seed catalog will discuss the hardiness of each plant, as well as diseases or conditions that affect or prevent its growth. The catalog will also give you a lot of planting information, including how to plant, how much heat and sun is required, the number of days it takes for the plant to mature, and what the plant should look like when it's ready to be harvested.

Armed with a couple of seed catalogs and the USDA Plant Hardiness Zone Map on p. 150, you and your children can begin to explore the kinds of plants that can grow well in your garden. Identify your particular hardiness zone and ask your children to choose plants from the catalogs that are labeled "hardy" for that zone. If necessary, explain to them why certain fruits or vegetables they choose may not do well in your climate.

Bush squash is low growing and compact, with many varieties reaching only 3 ft. to 4 ft. wide.

Peppers are available in many colors and add taste to salads, fajitas, and pasta.

It's fun to pick and eat sugar snap peas, pods and all.

Making a Plant List

With seed catalogs in hand, you and your children can begin to compile a plant list, which will eventually guide you in planting your most adventuresome garden ever (since becoming a parent, that is).

As I said before, it's important to choose vegetables and fruits your children will enjoy growing and eating. When making a plant list, be sure to pick a few plants that mature quickly so that the children will not lose interest in the garden (for more on quick-maturing vegetables, see the sidebar on the facing page). You should also make sure the plants you choose are *family* favorites—not just adult favorites. Over time, you can ask the children to expand their list of favorite vegetables and fruits, encouraging them to try different varieties of their most-liked plants.

Determining family favorites

Gather the family together with a couple of colorful, well-annotated, and photograph-filled seed catalogs and talk about which plants each family member wants to grow and eat (a perfect dinnertime conversation, by the way). Try to limit these gatherings to about a half hour so the children won't feel like it's work and won't get bored.

The catalogs you have looked at for years with academic interest can be a wondrous experience for your children. The pictures prompt them to ask about foods they have neither seen nor tasted. As a result, you may find yourself making a couple of research trips to a

GETTING A FAST START

When making the plant list for your garden, choose a few vegetables and fruits that will mature quickly because children can lose interest in a garden fast if nothing is happening. Also, if the children plant some quick-maturing vegetables and fruits, the wait for the slower-maturing plants, such as tomatoes, peppers, and melons, will not seem quite as long.

The vegetables in the chart at right will give you food on your plates anywhere from 25 to 60 days. The days shown represent the average number of days from seed sowing to maturity. Make sure the children keep planting after they harvest, especially with greens and radishes, so they will have a ready supply of gardening satisfaction just waiting for them.

QUICK-MATURING VEGETABLES	
Plant	Days to maturity
Beets	50
Broccoli	50 (from transplant)
Bush beans	50
Leaf lettuce	45
Peas (early varieties)	55
Radishes	25
Scallions	40
Spinach	50
Summer squash	48

fine grocer or, better yet, to an adventurous restaurant so that your children can discover firsthand the taste of sugar snap peas (imagine, eating the *pods*!), bush squash, melons, purple bush beans, hybrid corn, or other new vegetables and fruits.

Using the information in the catalogs as a reference, ask everyone to write or tell you what they would like to eat from a family garden. What you read or hear may surprise you. Parents may have fond memories of their grandparents' garden and may desire a long-lost taste sensation. For instance, my mother keeps pleading with me to plant okra, a favorite specialty on my grandmother's dinner table. Children may have seen a plant in a catalog that looks cool or tasted a fruit or vegetable that they enjoyed. If children are having trouble picking plants, ask them to choose a garden product they like to eat and then choose the plants that help

Purple bush beans are a colorful and flavorful addition to the dinner table. (Photo by Boyd Hagen.)

Tomatillos can be a wonderful surprise in a family garden, allowing your family to make fresh batches of salsa.

make that product. For instance, my family loves pesto, so we grow enough basil and garlic to last all year.

If a family discussion isn't fruitful, or if your dinnertime resembles the floor of a stock exchange, as my family's sometimes does, try another approach. Gather up your brood and take a fact-finding research trip to a fine grocer, a well-stocked whole-foods store, or a supermarket.

Give each child a couple of dollars and a seed catalog to use as a reference. Let all of the children know that they are to spend the money only on fruits or vegetables that they would like to grow in the family garden. Pass on these rules: No duplicates are allowed,

it's okay to buy just one of anything, and the fruit or vegetable must be able to be grown in your garden (check the catalogs for the plant's hardiness). Let the store or produce manager know what you are up to so that he or she may be of help, if necessary, and call ahead if you'll be shepherding a large group. Choose a quiet time for the store, like a weekday afternoon or evening, avoiding Saturdays at all cost. Challenge the children to come up with a vegetable that no one has ever heard of or that no one has ever tasted.

I tried this with my own children and with a group of 6- and 8-year-olds. The trip to the store provided us with gardening ideas, taste sensations, and numerous stories to take back to interested adults. It's also a terrific way to learn about the origins of fruits and vegetables that are out of season in your area, pesticides and preservatives that might be used, as well as the general availability of organic produce. Giving the children the power over their selections usually results in their tasting vegetables that no amount of pleading by parents could produce.

Expanding the list of family favorites

Once you have a list of vegetables and fruits that are family favorites, put it aside. Now the fun part begins: experimenting with new plant choices.

One of the most satisfying and enjoyable aspects of welcoming your children into your garden is the permission you instantly receive to try different things. For instance, children may decide that orange pumpkins are too plain compared to the white ones they see in a catalog. Or, perhaps, they want to grow funny-looking Baby carrots or popcorn.

Now you can begin to see the possibility of this year's garden being one of the most different and risky gardens you have ever planted. But don't get too wild. Even though your children may want to load the garden down with colorful plant varieties, remember that you want them to eat a good amount of what they plant, not just look at it. Take advantage of your children's choices, but try to keep reality in sight. Steer them toward colorful variations of the family's favorite vegetables and fruits or toward

new crops that they'd like to try and that will grow in your climate.

I search out catalogs and farmers for seeds and seedlings of different varieties of our favorites, so, as a family, we'll never tire of our garden. I also choose a few surprises each year, such as purple cauliflower, white eggplant, tomatillos, beets with brilliant pink and white rings inside, homegrown popcorn, miniature pumpkins, and yellow and sweet chocolate peppers.

Not all of these have been palatable hits. No one but me would eat the cauliflower, not because of the color

My son Seth shows off his cherry-tomato crop. This bowl ended up as his snack during a showing of one of his favorite movies.

but because no one liked the taste. Eggplant was only eaten in parmigiana form, which is a rather heavy meal to have several times a week in late summer. We had so many tomatillos that all the batches of salsa in the world wouldn't use even half of them. And my sons couldn't imagine eating beets until some persistent coaxing proved to them that beets—which they learned was an alternative source of sugar—were sweet. However, my sons only tried the beets once because they turned their tongues bright pink (a girl's color!), and consequently, I ate beets every other day, in various forms, for the next several weeks.

Nevertheless, the popcorn was a complete success, both in terms of taste and pure growing satisfaction, the pumpkins were lots of fun for holiday decorating, and the peppers appeared in funky colors and were tasty in salads, in fajitas, and over pasta.

Combining family favorites with new plant choices

After adding new vegetables and fruits to your list of family favorite plants, you probably have the makings for a very large garden. I find that it's best to choose six or seven fruits and vegetables from your list of family favorites and add two or three more from your list of "experimental" plants.

A small garden is usually large enough to grow a significant number of vegetables and fruits but small enough to be maintained and harvested easily. Obviously, the number of plants you grow will depend on the amount of time and space you can devote to the garden (I'll talk more about garden size and layout in Chapter 2). If you have more time or space, are an experienced gardener, or have lots of children to satisfy, choose more plants and load up your garden plot.

Perfect Plants for a Family Garden

I introduced my two sons, Bennett and Seth, to the wonders of gardening by growing three vegetables they like to eat—cucumbers, carrots, and tomatoes. Then I gradually experimented with new varieties of their favorites and added new plants each year.

Let me introduce you to these three plants and a few others that may work well for your family garden. They are all fairly easy to grow and offer a wide variety of maturing times so that your garden will provide a steady stream of produce all summer long.

Cucumbers

To intrigue both of my sons—who, by the way, are over seven years apart in age—we have tried planting at least one new cucumber variety each season. The three varieties my children enjoy most are slicing, pickling, and Oriental.

Slicing cucumbers are popular with children because they look just like the ones at the supermarket (and taste three times better). Mid East, or Beit Alpha, slicing cucumbers are best for salads and should be picked when they reach about 4 in. to 5 in. long to ensure perfect flavor and texture. American slicing cucumbers can grow bigger, to about 9 in., without losing quality. Watch your children's eyes as they uncover one of these slicing cucumbers in the garden and then wait for them to ask whether the fruit really came from the local supermarket.

Although slicing cucumbers take about 58 days to mature, including a plant or two in your garden will be fun for the whole family. They do, however, seem to attract striped cucumber beetles more than other varieties, so you may need to put in a little extra effort to keep them pest free.

Pickling cucumbers are often children's favorites because they are small, easy to pick, fairly quick to grow at 48 to 55 days to maturity, and delicious to eat right off the vine. For late-summer pickling projects, these cucumbers should be harvested when they are about 2 in. in length.

Oriental cucumbers are sweet, curved in shape with high ridges, and take only 60 days to mature. They often grow up to 15 in. long, are very tolerant of hot weather, and make terrific pickles. Of course, the overall favorite was the long, curved "burpless" cucumber, the name of which my sons try repeatedly to discredit.

Carrots

Carrots can be grown by just about anyone, as long as the soil has been well prepared (for more on soil preparation, see Chapter 4), and maintaining a bed of carrots involves just weeding and some thinning. I like to grow both slow- and quick-maturing varieties (which are typically long and short, respectively).

Carrots are underground surprises for children, who find the digging part to be tons of fun.

The long varieties that my family likes are the Nantes and Imperator carrots. Nantes carrots are long, averaging 7 in. to 8 in., and mature in 70 days or more (some early varieties mature at 6 in. in 55 to 60 days). All Nantes carrots are known for their sweet, crisp presentation. Nantes carrots hold their flavor and moisture well in cooler temperatures and so are perfect for storage and fall crops.

Imperator carrots are the longest for which you will probably find seeds. They are a delight to grow with children, as long as your children are blessed with patience. Imperator carrots will take at least 68 to 72 days to mature, but pulling a 9-in. carrot from the ground is a guaranteed showstopper for young children. Imperator carrots hold their flavor

across a picture of celery. The picture intrigued me, so I ordered a very small packet of seeds and started some seedlings. What a find! The plant was fascinating to watch grow and mature, for both me *and* the children, and was quite an experience to harvest.

The taste, however, was to behold. The celery taste with which we often are acquainted through celery salt or celery seed can't stand up to fresh celery. The plant required little attention throughout its 80-day growth period and was crisp, free of thick strings, and bursting with a full, smooth flavor. Next season, my family will start a plant every three days for a couple of weeks so we can extend our celery-eating season. We're hooked!

Sweet corn

The same season my family tried growing celery, we tried growing super-sweet, bicolor corn. We had only one problem: We didn't grow enough to satisfy our cravings. Since sweet corn can mature anywhere from 65 to 92 days from planting, depending on the variety, we should have planted a number of varieties with various maturity dates so that we could have harvested corn over a six-week period.

Plant the corn on the northern side of your garden so that the sun casts the corn shadows away from the other plants. Use a high-phosphate starter when planting the seeds, and keep your planting soil good and moist—corn is a very thirsty vegetable to grow. Harvest the corn on time to prevent the kernels from losing their sweetness, and refrigerate your harvested ears if you are not going to use them immediately—the cool storage will help preserve the sugars in the kernels.

Melons

The corn was a success the first try, but it took a couple of garden seasons to find just the right melon for my cool, New England climate.

At first, the boys and I started the seedlings too late to satisfy their need for instant gratification and to give the fruit enough time to ripen. The boys picked the melon well before it was ready—even though it looked like the ones in the market—and they were

You can conserve space by growing climbing plants on trellises. In this garden, melons climb a tripod trellis made from bamboo garden stakes and twine.

disappointed. The next season we planted butterscotch melons, which take only 75 days to mature, and we were presented with a small but sweet fruit, with brightly streaked orange and green flesh. Butterscotch melons are delicious and fun to cut into. Melons can take up a lot of space if left to grow on the ground. To conserve space, train the melons to grow up a trellis.

Lettuce and other leafy greens

Over the past three seasons, my family's collective love of salad has nudged us from basic green- and red-leaf lettuce (which take about 46 to 60 days to mature) to heads of crisp romaine and any mesclun mix we can find, from spicy to mild.

The romaine lettuce takes about a week longer than green- and red-leaf lettuce to mature, but it's worth the wait if you have Caesar salad fans in your family. Arugula, chard, mache, and mesclun mixes, however, can be harvested when very young, some as early as 40 days. A spring salad of these greens alone is a signal to my family that summer is on the way.

Now my family can't imagine eating commercial lettuce when we can have a mesclun mix 8 months out of the year, thanks to early and late plantings (I'll talk more about planting in Chapter 5).

Broccoli

My family has grown broccoli for the past three years. It is easy to grow, displays bright green leaves, and takes about 50 to 65 days to mature.

The broccoli was a hit because it was still growing heartily in September and October, having survived the first several frosts in mid-October. The only problem we had with the broccoli was green cabbage worms, which were difficult to control because they blend in perfectly with the leaves of the plant (fortunately, the worms won't survive an early frost in the fall).

Sugar snap peas

Sugar snap peas are a gift to parents. They are crunchy, sweet, easy to grow, and mature in about 55 days from the seed planting date. Children delight in picking the pod and popping it whole into their mouths. These peas make an early appearance in my family's May salads and lunch boxes and continue throughout the summer and fall thanks to successive plantings.

Potatoes

Potatoes are one of those vegetables, like celery, that children seldom associate with a garden. They are, though, fun to plant and easy to grow. Although large, full-sized potatoes take up to 90 or 100 days to mature, baby potatoes can be harvested in about 60 days. Snap a picture of your children's faces as they push the soil away from the base of the potato plants and discover handfuls of baby potatoes attached to the roots. Your job is then to convince them to eat the potatoes in a form other than fried. Good luck, and pass the ketchup!

CHAPTER TWO

Laying Out the Garden

garden will determine whether or not the plants will grow and produce, so it's important to put some time and effort into this planning phase.

The Garden Size

The biggest trap many family gardeners fall into is creating a garden that is too large. Even though you may have the best of intentions, over time a garden that is too large will become a maintenance nightmare.

My family, like many others, has eagerly planted large gardens only to cut back slowly on the time dedicated to gardening. Sometime in September, we have ended up with a garden full of overripened fruit and out-of-control, overgrown plantings. This situation is not enjoyable for adult gardeners, let alone for children. Most children (and many adults) won't enjoy spending their warm sunny days tending an overgrown garden plot.

When thinking about the size of your family garden, encourage the children to be realistic. Work with them to plan the size according to the time the family can devote to the garden. Also have them think about the purpose of the garden and the amount of space needed to plant the vegetables and fruits on the family's plant list.

Planting the garden is easier if you and your children create a plan before heading outside.

Once you and your family have decided what to plant, the time has come to settle on the size and location of your garden so that you can draw up a garden plan. The size of your garden will determine how much attention the plot will get from you and your family. The garden location will dictate the amount of sun, water, and nutrients your plants will get. Ultimately, both the size and location of the

The family meeting is a great time to choose plants for the garden.

Time considerations

It's family meeting time. Everyone's excited about the garden project and is expecting luscious vegetables simply to appear on their plates beginning mid-July. Time for a reality check. A garden is fun, but every foot of it requires attention—from planting and watering to hoeing and mulching—throughout the entire season.

At this family meeting, it's important to ask everyone this question: How much time do you want to devote to your garden? You may have thousands of square feet at your disposal but may have only evenings and weekends to spend on gardening, and even those times may be shared with other home, community, and parental responsibilities. Your children may also have other commitments, such as summer camp, baseball and soccer games, swimming, or just spending time with friends. Because of these time constraints on both parents and children, don't plan a garden that will be overwhelming in size.

To get an idea of how much time each family member has to devote to the garden, you need to decide right from the beginning what the family duties are going to be. Gardening is a lot of work, and everyone needs to pitch in, whether for weeding, watering, or harvesting (I'll talk more about garden maintenance in Chapter 6).

Have your children sign up for gardening duties they may enjoy. I am

Every foot of a garden requires maintenance, from planting and watering to hoeing and mulching.

one of the curious types of gardeners who happens to enjoy weeding (really, I do). Most children, however, tend not to enjoy this tedious chore. But they do love to play with water and hoses, so watering comes as a natural outgrowth of these interests.

Because watering should be done in the early morning or evening (to avoid moisture lost to evaporation), the job can revolve around your children's activities—like before or after day camp. It's also a terrific way for children to cool off after a hot day in the sun. (If you are working in the garden while your children are watering, expect to get wet!)

You also need to encourage the children to get involved in other garden maintenance. Children seem to enjoy using tools, so buy them some small,

sturdy gardening tools and gloves. With their own tools in hand, children will be more apt to help you keep the garden neat and the soil loose and weed free. Come harvest time, the tools will allow the children to take part in the harvesting—which is the real treat for them.

Once your children have signed up for their own gardening duties and you have an idea of how much time they want to devote to the garden, take a look at your own schedule. If one parent (or both) either has much of the summer off, due to a career in education, or is at home for most of the day and is willing to dedicate a few hours each day to the garden, then your family could plan and build a large garden. In many households, however, this is not the case.

For instance, as much as I love to garden, I also work full time and have only evenings and weekends to devote to gardening. And even these gardening times are worked around family and church obligations, beach visits, camping trips, and other summer activities. Consequently—although I get help from my sons—I have time to plant and maintain just three small (8-ft. by 8-ft.) beds jammed full of vegetables and fruits. And even this small garden, which totals less that 200 sq. ft., can sometimes be a grand effort in a hot and dry summer, especially when special projects might pop up at work. So be realistic, and plan your garden's size according to the time you and your children can devote to the project.

If you have a busy family, consider gardening in raised beds, which are easy to maintain. (Photo by Helen Albert.)

What's the purpose?

Once you have an idea of how much time your family can and will dedicate to a garden, think about the purpose of your garden. How you expect the garden to meet your family's needs and what plants you include in the garden will directly affect how much space you must devote to it.

For instance, a small salad garden, with a modest assortment of greens, radishes, scallions, herbs, and perhaps a tomato plant or two, can take up a very small space—as compact as a 6-ft. by 6-ft. plot—immediately outside your kitchen door. If you simply want to provide your family with fresh produce throughout the summer, with no surplus intended for winter storage, freezing, or canning, your garden size can probably be as small as 120 sq. ft.

But if your intent is to reduce your dependence on outside food sources as much as possible, you may need a garden as large as 250 sq. ft. A garden this big will allow you to grow enough produce to store for the entire winter.

Also affecting the size of your garden are the plants you choose and the spacing they require. You can grow bush varieties of beans and squash and trellis certain plants, such as tomatoes and cucumbers, to maximize the space in a small garden. But if you and your children decide to grow a large number of giant pumpkins, rows and rows of 10-in. carrots, and 25 zucchini plants, a huge amount of space will be required. A quality seed catalog will give you terrific advice on space requirements for particular plants. However,

MAKING PLANT DATA SHEETS

Seed catalogs are a great source of information about the plants you and your children want to grow in your garden. But when you need to access that information, such as the number of days to maturity or the spacing between plants, you have to flip through the catalog pages to find the specifics for each plant. An easier method is to compile a plant data sheet for each of the plants in the garden. The plant data sheets help organize the plant information so that you and your children can accurately plan the size and location of the garden. The sheets will also come in handy as your children begin to draw the garden plan on paper (a sample plant data sheet is shown at left).

Compiling the plant data sheets is a vigorous project that accomplishes much toward a successful garden. Along the way, the children will learn about the important roles that geography, light, heat, and moisture play in the growth of the plants. Of course, the amount of organization and research help you'll need to provide will depend on the size of your family and on the ages of your children.

SAMPLE PLANT DATA SHEET

Plant name: _Sun Gold cherry tomato_   Seed or (Seedling?)
(circle one)

Date for planting: _June 1st_   Days to maturity: _57 days_

Temp. for planting: _70° days_ _45°+ nights_   Temp. for harvest: _75°-80°_

Best climate/exposure: _warm, southern_ How much sun?: _full sun_

Method of planting: *(check one)*   Spacing between plants:

Rows _____   _____

Hills _____   _____

Trellis _____   _____

Stakes _✓_   _14 to 20 inches_

Alternate/additional planting dates: _throughout June_

Other information: _Harvest when tangerine color. Indeterminate plant needs staking or tomato cage. Very tall vines! The fruit will split if overripe. Watch for flea beetles throughout the season._

Begin by passing out seed packets and catalogs to the children. Divide the plants up evenly among the children while keeping some for yourself. Then ask the children to gather the following data:

- initial planting conditions, either by direct seeding or by seedling
- date for planting (which will depend on whether you direct seed or transplant seedlings)
- number of days to maturity
- temperature for planting
- temperature for harvesting
- the preferred climate or amount of light or heat the plant needs (lettuce, for instance, can survive well in some filtered sun or in a cooler spot than tomatoes or peppers can)
- method of planting (rows vs. hills)
- spacing between plants
- alternate or additional planting dates, if any
- other information, such as common pests to watch for, special nutrient requirements, the color and size of the mature fruit, or other interesting tips

repeatedly going back to the catalogs can, at times, be a nuisance. An easier way to keep track of all the necessary information for planting is to create a plant data sheet for each of your plant choices (see the sidebar at left).

The Garden Location

As in real estate, it's location, location, location when it comes to having a successful garden. A well-located garden can enable you and your children to make the most efficient use of your space *and* time and can greatly enhance the enjoyment of gardening as a family. You need to keep the garden away from areas that could harm the plants but close to a water source. You must also pick a spot that will receive adequate airflow and sunshine.

Bring the children outside and have them look around for the perfect spot for the garden. This is a fun activity, will help the children learn some basic geography and science, and will encourage some ownership in the garden. First, have the children locate possible sources of harm to the garden, using the list on p. 25 for reference. The garden should not be located near these areas.

Then remind the children that they need a source for water so that watering may be done easily. They won't want to roll out and roll up 100 ft. of hose every day to water the garden (and you won't, either). For convenience, you may want the garden to be near the compost pile or close to your gardening shed (if you have either).

The garden location should also receive adequate airflow, so be sure the plot is not obstructed completely. Airflow is important for pollination, and it allows heat and moisture to flow around the plants so that they don't bake or receive too much moisture.

Sunshine is also extremely important for healthy plant growth, so choose a

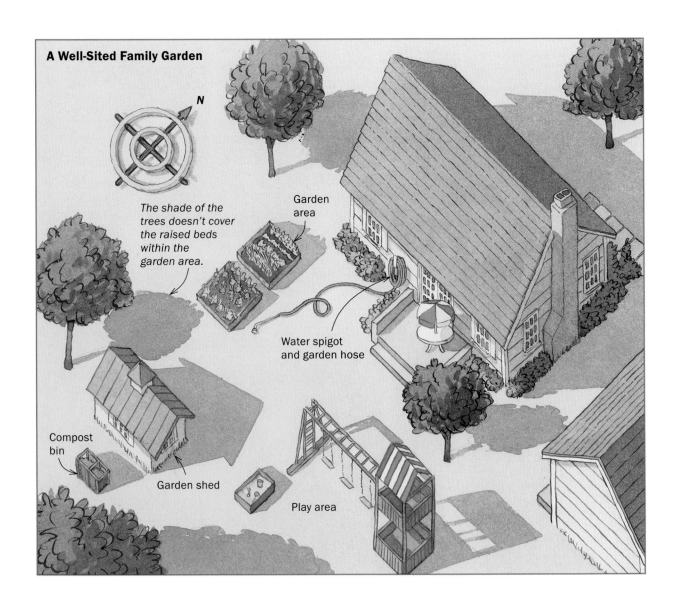

A Well-Sited Family Garden

N

The shade of the trees doesn't cover the raised beds within the garden area.

Garden area

Water spigot and garden hose

Compost bin

Garden shed

Play area

sunny spot for the garden. On a sunny day, go into the yard with your children. Explain to them that a garden needs a minimum of 6 hours of direct sun daily to flourish (although 8 to 10 hours is better). With a compass in hand, help them locate the north, south, east, and west areas of the yard. (Make sure the children record the compass directions. They'll need this information to draw the garden plan.) Tell them that the southern and western parts of the yard are most likely to receive the most direct sunlight and are the prime areas to locate the garden. If building a garden in the south or west parts of your yard is not possible, help the children locate a plot with sufficient light, little shade, and as much airflow as possible.

Siting the garden on your land is the perfect time for you to teach your children basic compass skills.

DON'T GARDEN NEAR THESE AREAS

- **Streets or driveways:** Fumes from cars can rob plants of valuable oxygen.
- **Swingsets:** One out-of-control child and your tender seedlings will be trampled underfoot.
- **Oil or propane tanks:** Even the smallest spill or leak can kill plants and contaminate soil.
- **Heavily treed areas:** Garden-loving animals lurk here, just waiting to munch on tender sprouting plants. If you can't avoid this location, don't forget the fence!
- **Swimming pools:** Chlorine in pool water kills plants, and when kids and pools mix, water is bound to be splashed around.
- **Large trees:** Their roots will overpower the garden, taking necessary water and nutrients, and the shade could rob the garden of needed sunshine.

The Garden Plan

Once you and your family have settled on the ideal size and location for the garden, it's time to put your plans on paper.

Drawing the garden plan involves a good dose of creativity and imagination for the children. Sometimes, however, our own need for perfection turns a delightful activity into a stressful undertaking for both parent and child. The first and only rule: relax and have fun with the plan. As long as the plant drawings are labeled, corn can look like pears, and carrots can look like corn. The key to the garden plan is placing the right plant in the right place. With some general direction from you, your children will create an artistic masterpiece that will serve as a map when they begin planting and as a wall decoration once they have finished.

Before beginning the garden plan, take your children to buy some drawing supplies. You'll need a good array of washable markers, crayons, or colored pencils (which are ideal because they are erasable), as well as the plant data sheets you compiled earlier.

I also suggest investing a couple of dollars in some high-quality engineering graph paper (with ⅛-in. or ¼-in. grids), which has a heavier weight than the graph paper sold at your local drug store. The engineering graph paper is a good choice for children who are about 10 to 13 years old. For children younger than that, you might want to buy a tablet of flip-chart graph paper, which is large (usually 27 in. by 34 in.), with 1-in. or 2-in. grids. Because their fine motor skills are not well developed, younger children tend to write large with broader motions. The flip-chart graph paper can easily accommodate their big drawings. Engineering graph paper and flip-chart paper are available at most office-supply stores. If you have very young children, a simpler way to make the garden plan is to create a felt garden plan (see the sidebar on the facing page).

If your children are very young, say 6 to 8 years old, you may want to use an easel. I have found that children in this age group like to work on their garden plan while standing up. Flip-chart graph paper can be ripped out of the tablet easily and can be placed on an easel.

Drawing the plan

Once you have all the necessary drawing materials, you and your children can settle in and begin working on the garden plan.

The first step is to go outside with a tape measure and your children and measure the size of the garden. If you have a garden consisting of a few individual beds, measure each one as well as the entire garden.

After taking the measurements, decide on a scale for the plan. The scale will depend on the size of the garden and on the size of the paper you have chosen. If you are using engineering graph paper, a good scale is ½ in. = 1 ft. If you are using flip-chart graph paper with younger children, a manageable scale is 2 in. = 1 ft. By the way, it's okay if the children don't draw exactly to

Children ages 3 to 5 often bring a pure sense of innocence and wonder to gardening, but they are often excluded from the planning activities described in this chapter because of their not-yet-developed fine motor and reading skills. A felt garden plan is the perfect solution, allowing these young children to participate in the planning process.

This "feltscaping" project requires a piece of ¼-in. plywood (about 2 ft. by 3 ft.), a stapler, scissors, and pieces of felt: brown (light and dark), red, yellow, white, blue, and green are the basic colors you'll need.

Begin by cutting a piece of brown felt about 3 in. larger than the plywood. Place the felt on a table, smooth it, and then place the plywood on the felt, roughly centered. Pull the felt taut around the plywood and staple it

to the back, as shown in the left drawing below.

Now, have the children cut out various objects to be included in the garden, such as the sun, clouds, trees, fences, a compass, and birds, as well as depictions of the plants to be placed in the garden. (The children may need your help with these jobs, depending on their ages and skill levels.) And don't forget worms, bugs, bees, and slugs, which are important additions to the garden and will help you introduce the concepts of organic gardening to your youngest horticulturists. The children can place these items on the felt plan, as shown in the right drawing below.

If you want to get fancy, cover some of the root crops (such as carrots, potatoes, and radishes) with brown felt. When it's time to

"harvest" these crops, remove the brown felt, revealing the mature plants below.

You can do something similar for other fruits and vegetables. For instance, say you have planted tomatoes in the garden. Cut out the leafy green portion of the plant and place it on the felt board. Come harvest time, add a bunch of yellow or red fruit to the stalk. You could even show the phases of growth, allowing the children to place first green, then pale-orange, and finally bright-red tomatoes on the plant as harvest nears.

By recording the dates of these growth changes, the children will gain a basic understanding of the growing process and the timing involved. The felt garden plan can be used year after year until your children are old enough to take on more difficult gardening tasks.

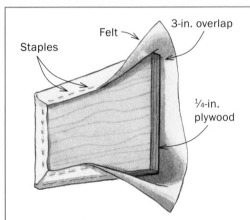

Attaching the felt
Cut a piece of brown felt about 3 in. larger than the plywood. Place the felt on a table, smooth it, and then roughly center the plywood on the felt. Pull the felt taut around the plywood and staple it to the back.

Adding the plants
Have the children cut out the objects to be included in the garden, then place these items on the felt plan.

A carefully drawn plan can give children an easy reference from which to plant the garden.

as parsnips and leeks, should be located on the perimeter of the garden, away from frequently turned-over or harvested beds so that the plants can mature undisturbed. Try to get the children to "marry" some plants together to take advantage of all the protective benefits of companion planting (for more on companion planting, see Chapter 6).

Heat-loving plants, such as melons, peppers, and tomatoes, need to be in the warmer parts of the garden (the south and west areas). Cool-loving plants, such as lettuce, spinach, and peas, on the other hand, should be placed in the north and east areas. The plant data sheets will allow the children to find this information easily. To make this research more fun, treat it like a treasure hunt. For instance, put the data sheets for heat-loving plants in one pile and cool-loving plants in another. Let the children mix and match the plants to create their very own garden areas.

Next, have the children write the names of the plants where they will be located roughly on the plan. Consult the plant data sheets to find out whether the plant needs to be staked or trellised, the spacing information, and any other important details. With the basic research finished, the children can then start drawing.

The drawing of the garden plan is an exciting activity, particularly if you encourage the children to be as creative as possible. Begin by having the children sketch any garden features, such as paths, stepping stones, or birdbaths, that will be included in the garden.

scale. Try to coach them and teach them, but don't take over the process in an attempt to get the drawing exact.

Have the children draw in the garden perimeter as close to scale as possible using a black marker or pencil. Then draw in the compass directions they recorded earlier.

Before adding the plants to the plan, have a discussion with the children about what should go where. Prompt them to remember that tall, mature plants, such as corn, can shade out low-growing crops, so the taller plants should be placed on the north or west sides of the garden to lessen the amount of shadows they cast (see the sample garden plan on the facing page).

Mention that long-term crops (those that take a long time to mature), such

Sample Garden Plan

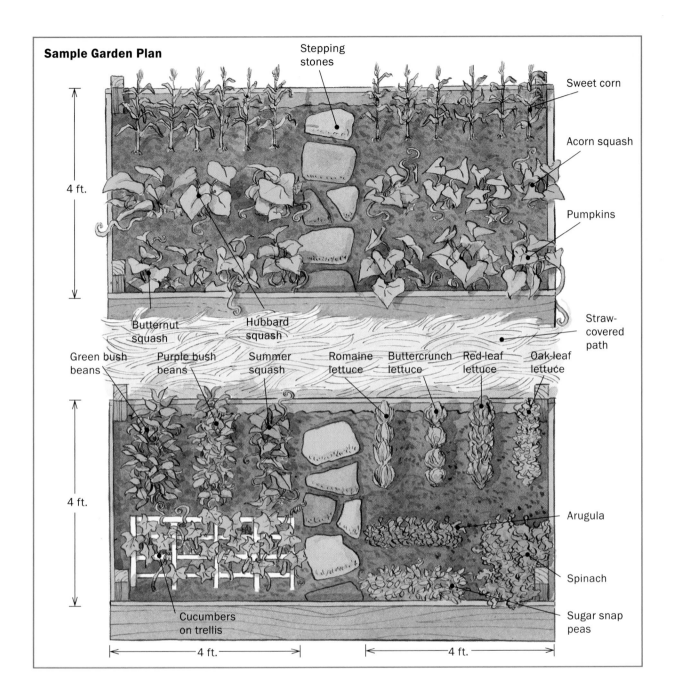

Stepping stones

Sweet corn

Acorn squash

Pumpkins

Straw-covered path

4 ft.

Butternut squash

Hubbard squash

Green bush beans

Purple bush beans

Summer squash

Romaine lettuce

Buttercrunch lettuce

Red-leaf lettuce

Oak-leaf lettuce

4 ft.

Arugula

Spinach

Sugar snap peas

Cucumbers on trellis

4 ft.

4 ft.

Suggest that the children draw one vegetable or fruit at a time, concentrating on spacing the plant with the others in the garden. Use the plant data sheets for reference and the grids on the paper as a way to judge distance. Pencil in a small black box (which I call a data box) next to each planting. This box should be big enough to accommodate some planting and harvesting data. The

A well-thought-out garden plan helps ensure success while showing your children the science, math, and creativity involved in gardening.

data boxes can be updated or revised as the season progresses and can be consulted for next year's planning.

Drawing and placing the plants on the garden plan may be too tedious or too reliant on fine motor skills for some children, particularly for those who prefer to design rather than to deal with data. You can ask these children to design a special border or a sign or logo for the garden plan, while giving the more precise and technically inclined children the responsibilities of determining the spacing and placing of the plants.

The key is to get the children to draw the plan while not limiting their creativity. Let the children sketch flying or nesting birds, fences, nearby houses or gardening sheds, benches,

and flowers—anything that allows them to express their own excitement and the beauty of the gardening season while completing the very important garden plan.

As a side project (hopefully after the real garden plan is nearly completed), ask the children to design a garden of the future or a garden on another planet. Let them go wild. Based on my personal experience, graph paper seems to lead to the designing of high-tech weaponry, no matter how interested in gardening my sons are. One year, I suggested that the boys design a garden on Mars, including any far-out garden implements—rocket powered, perhaps—that would be used in it as well as the Martian gardeners and the plants they might grow. Use your imagination to keep the project going and interest high.

Filling in the plant data boxes

Once the all the elements in the garden have been drawn in and colored, the children should fill in each plant data box. Include the planting date for each variety of plant (direct-to-seeding date or transplant date) and the days to maturity or estimated harvest date. The plant data box is also a handy place to note any succession crop that you will plant once the first crop is harvested (for more on succession planting, see Chapter 6).

Displaying the plan

Once the garden plan has been finished, you can hang it on a wall or bulletin board for display, preferably near the door to the backyard so that the children can consult it at a moment's notice. If your plan was drawn on small graph paper, make a copy of the plan for each child and adult participating in this project. Then laminate the original plan to protect the colors and detail that have been so carefully placed on it.

Keeping track of changes

Changes to a garden plan are common. For instance, seedlings you planned to purchase might be unavailable or difficult to find, one row of carrots just may not seem enough, or your garden may shrink in size due to hidden tree roots or boulders. (If you laminated the original plan, you won't be able to make changes to it, so keep a copy

nearby, in a protective folder, on which the children can record changes in colored pencil or marker.)

After the season is over, and the garden is put to bed for the winter, call a family meeting to compare the data on the original plan with the actual activity. Ask the children to note the changes and identify why they were made. This discussion can lead to fascinating observations about the weather, climate, soil conditions, or pest and disease problems that can assist you and the children in planning for the following season's garden. Ask one child to be the record keeper for these discussions so that you capture all of the information and observations. These records can eventually become a gardening journal for the children.

These discussions don't necessarily have to take place at the end of the season, however. Feel free to gather the family together during the summer to talk about how the garden project is moving along. Remember to keep records so you have a written history of the project.

Building the Garden

The loose, deep soil in a raised bed drains well and warms quickly, nurturing the vegetables and fruits. (Photo by Scott Phillips.)

Many adult gardeners suffer from spring fever, which begins for some as early as mid-February. When you have children involved in a garden project, the fever can become an epidemic. By the time early spring rolls around, the children may be frustrated by the lack of snow to play in and the lack of outdoor activities available to them. Luckily, a garden is an ideal way for both parents and children to go outside and get dirty.

If you and your children locate the garden, choose plants, and draw up the plan during the winter, in March and April you'll be ready to start building the garden as soon as the earth is soft and manageable. At the same time you should be working the soil (see Chapter 4) and starting seeds (see Chapter 5). In this chapter I'll talk about why a raised-bed garden works well for children, and I'll illustrate how you and your children can have fun building one.

Advantages of Raised-Bed Gardening

When many people first contemplate building a garden, they expect simply to dig up a plot of soil, plop in a few rows of seedlings, water, and then wait, perhaps throwing in some commercial fertilizer guaranteed to produce gargantuan produce. But this basic row garden is not ideal for a child-friendly garden. I prefer instead to garden with my children in raised beds, in which the garden is divided into rectangular planting beds that are built up higher than the surrounding soil in the yard.

Raised-bed gardens are perfect for introducing children to the thrills of gardening because they allow for well-defined planting areas and wide paths, efficient use of amendments and fertilizers, and well-draining and warm planting areas. They're also appropriate for almost any type of plant.

Well-defined planting areas

A raised-bed garden eliminates many of the problems associated with row gardening, making planting and garden maintenance easier for the children (as well as for the adults). It allows you to cut down on wasted space and gives the children a well-defined area in which to work, eliminating any fears of not doing the right thing in the right place.

For instance, having a series of raised beds in one garden plot allows different

Wood, brick, or natural stone can be used to frame a raised bed, and paths can be made of stone, gravel, mulch, or even grass. (Photo by Lefever/Grushow from Grant Heilman Photography.)

groups of children—or each child—to have their own garden. Younger children are able to plant easy, quick-maturing vegetables and play in the dirt at the same time, while older children can create decorative patterns for their plantings, design luscious borders, and attempt more adventurous or unique plantings, such as various chili peppers, heirloom tomatoes, or antique herbs.

My raised beds are not as "raised" as some, but they fit well just outside my back kitchen door and are easy for my family to work in.

Dividing a row garden in this manner is difficult at best and can easily lead to conflicts if one child gets in the way of another.

A row garden does not make the most efficient use of the space available because you have to allow for paths between each row, which can take up a considerable amount of what could otherwise be cultivated areas. And when children walk—or stomp—on these paths, they will become compacted and unsuitable for planting the following year without a lot of labor (even if they are covered by mulch). And remember that children may not yet have sharp motor skills, so navigating a narrow path between rows can be difficult and frustrating for them.

A raised-bed garden allows for slightly wider paths because there are fewer of them than in a row garden. The paths can be easily navigated by children and give them easy access to the beds without their worrying about stepping into planting areas.

Efficient use of amendments and fertilizers

More important than these issues, however, is the fact that working the soil in a raised-bed garden is easier. A raised-bed garden allows space for a deep layer of fertile topsoil and conserves the amount of amendments and fertilizer you must add because you are feeding just the areas within the beds, not the pathways or border areas. With a row garden, on the other hand,

you work the entire planting bed. Consequently, you'll waste a lot of amendments and fertilizer in the paths between rows and surrounding borders that will not be planted (not to mention the amount of time you'll waste working these areas!).

I know exactly the condition of the soil in each of my raised beds because I have added soil amendments that are appropriate for the plants that will be living in a particular bed. For instance, I plant acid-loving plants, such as potatoes, where I have added soil amendments to increase the acidity and plant the rest of the vegetables (which require only slightly acid soil) in other beds (for more on acid and alkaline soils, see Chapter 4). This would be difficult to accomplish in a row garden.

I feel confident that whatever I plant will grow well. And when the plants grow, your children's gardening experience will be satisfying and will make them feel like accomplished and proud gardeners.

Well-draining, warm planting areas

The fact that the beds are raised ensures that the soil will drain well and that the temperature will remain warm throughout the season. With a row garden, the soil is virtually level with the surrounding yard, which gives water a better chance of sitting on the surface for long periods. Stagnant water can rot stems, drown roots, and attract unwelcome pests such as slugs.

The soil in a raised bed usually stays about 6°F to 10°F warmer than the soil at ground level, which allows plants to sprout quickly and establish a strong root base early on. On the other hand, the soil within a row garden may take a long time to warm in the spring, which means plants will take a long time to grow. And the longer children have to wait for something to happen in the garden, the more likely they will find other, more quickly gratifying activities with which to occupy themselves (such as television).

Appropriate for almost any type of plant

Some gardeners use raised beds only for select crops, delegating vining crops, such as winter squash and pumpkins, trellised crops, such as pole beans and tomatoes, and tall plants, such as corn, to conventional row planting schemes. These plants are seen as being too tall

(corn or trellised plants) or taking up too much space, which pumpkins and squash certainly can do. However, I think you can grow almost any plant in a raised bed, as long as you plan the garden layout carefully.

For instance, my family's pumpkins share a bed with lettuce and spinach, but we allowed plenty of room around the pumpkin plants to accommodate the wandering vines. By the time we're ready to harvest the first plantings of lettuce and spinach, we have a good idea where the pumpkin vines are headed and can plant the second crop of greens around them. It's also acceptable to grow trellised (or staked) or tall plants in a raised bed, as long as you don't allow the crops to overshadow others in the bed, robbing the low-growing plants of valuable sunshine.

In a raised-bed garden, the soil dries out quickly following the spring thaw and is ready to work in late March.

Designing and Building a Raised-Bed Garden

Designing and constructing a raised-bed garden is easy, can accommodate any child of any age, and is a perfect way to get the whole family working as a team. When building a raised-bed garden, first consider the size and height of the beds and the width of the paths.

Sizing the beds and paths

The most important consideration is how large to make the beds and paths between them (if any).

The size of each bed (and how many are required) can be easily determined as long as the garden plan has been done accurately (see Chapter 2). The size will, in part, be determined by the number of plants you and your children have decided to grow and how much space is needed for each variety (for this information, consult the plant data sheets you and the children compiled during the winter). But perhaps the most important issue is designing each bed to be accessible. A raised bed should be designed so that the children can easily reach the middle without

A garden area can become a quiet retreat for family members. (Photo by Scott Phillips.)

Planting areas in a raised bed should be easy for children to reach.

children, the more successful your children's gardening will be.

A good general width for a bed is 4 ft., which should be sufficient for most children to reach into easily for planting, tending, and harvesting (the length will depend on the size of your garden). If you have very small children and beds wider than 4 ft., you may have to locate their plants closer to the edges.

Typically, raised beds are anywhere from 6 in. to 24 in. above ground level. The height will depend on how much amendments, such as manure or compost, you need to add to the soil and on the children's heights. (For instance, smaller children will have a more difficult time reaching into a bed if the frame is too high.)

If your garden is to have paths between beds, be sure they are wide enough to accommodate the number of children who will be working in the garden. Paths should be at least 1 ft. wide. If you are working with a large group of children, say more than four or five, it might be a good idea to make the paths at least 3 ft. wide to avoid bumps and pushes that can create chaos and turf battles within the garden.

having to step into the bed, making planting, tending, and cultivating the bed easy on their small hands.

Have the children take turns stretching their arms out and taking each other's measurements. If the children are close in size and age, the beds can all be the same size (simply base the size of the beds on the average arm length). But if there's a large disparity between the children's sizes and ages, it may be a good idea to let them make beds of various widths. Your children may even decide that they want to vary the size of their beds anyway, just to be different from siblings or friends. Or perhaps they want a different size bed for different age groups. If the children want to be different, let them go. Just keep reminding them to keep the beds accessible. The more this experience is personalized and directed by the

Choosing edging material for the beds

Raised beds are edged to provide support for the loosened soil and amendments that will be added. The beds may be edged simply by firming their sides in a slanted manner that is wider at the bottom; this technique is easy but is not best suited for young children. The temptation to dig close to the slant or to step on the edge is just

Building a Raised Bed

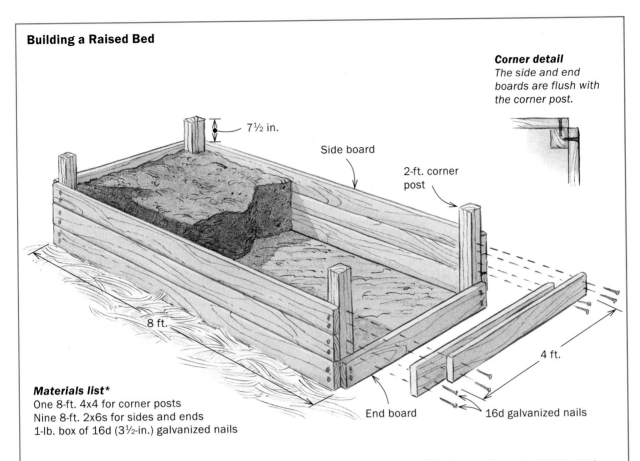

Corner detail
The side and end boards are flush with the corner post.

7½ in.

Side board

2-ft. corner post

8 ft.

4 ft.

End board

16d galvanized nails

Materials list*
One 8-ft. 4x4 for corner posts
Nine 8-ft. 2x6s for sides and ends
1-lb. box of 16d (3½-in.) galvanized nails

*The dimensions for this raised bed can be altered to fit your needs. Use wood that naturally resists insects and dry rot or that has been treated with a nonleaching formula so unwanted poisons do not touch the soil in the beds.

too great, and the confusion that a lack of an easily identified border creates leads to frustration, especially for the miniature perfectionists we all know and love. To avoid any of this confusion, I suggest framing the raised beds with wood.

There are a couple of ways to do this. The easiest method is to lay down 4x4 or 6x6 beams as the frame. The more complicated method is to nail a few 2x6s around four 4x4 corner posts (see the drawing above). Building the beds in this manner allows you to raise the soil up to a foot or two above ground level, which is particularly attractive to gardeners in areas of poor or heavy soil who need to add manure, compost, loam, or other organic matter to the bed so that plants will thrive.

But putting wood so close to the ground invites dry rot and termites, which could quickly turn your frame into mulch. If you want the wood to last, you need to choose a type that prohibits dry rot and insects.

Building a raised bed can be fun for children, especially the hammering part.

Unfortunately, that leaves you with two choices: expensive species, such as redwood or cedar, or treated wood.

Redwood or cedar contain a natural preservative and last several years before they begin to rot. The cost, for most of us, however, is prohibitive.

Wood that has been soaked in tar or creosote, such as traditional railroad ties, and pressure-treated wood (the green-colored stuff you usually see on decks) will last, without rot, for 10 years or more and is fairly reasonable in price. But the ingredient in both the tar and the pressure treatment that prevents the rotting is arsenic. Arsenic is a poison and not something you want in your garden or near your children. If you use traditional railroad ties or pressure-treated lumber, the arsenic in the wood will leach into your garden's soil, eventually reaching your vegetables.

Most garden centers and landscaping businesses now sell lumber that has been pressurized using a nonleaching process. Ask before you buy and request written information on the substance used to seal the wood.

When handling treated wood, wear gloves to keep the chemicals off. When cutting or sanding the material, wear a nuisance dust mask to keep the chemicals out of your lungs.

Framing the beds

If you have chosen to frame the beds with 4x4 or 6x6 beams, the installation is pretty simple. Work with the children to mark the location of the beams on the ground within each frame using string or chalk. Then give them trowels and have them dig a trench the same thickness as the beam and about 2 in. deep. This narrow trench will stabilize the frame almost instantly when the beams are placed inside it.

Now cut each beam to size, if necessary (this job is probably more suited for adults). A 4x4 can be cut with a sharp handsaw, but a bigger beam may require the use of a circular saw or a chainsaw. Be sure you are comfortable using the tool and follow all safety precautions (including wearing safety glasses). If you are uncomfortable with cutting lumber of this size, either design the beds to be larger—perhaps 8 ft. by 8 ft.—so that you can simply buy 8-ft. lengths or ask the lumberyard to cut the wood to length for you (you may be charged a small fee for this).

After the beams have been cut, help your children place them on the ground. To make the frame attractive and neat-looking, try to get each one flush with the adjoining one. You can use a level for this, or you can line up the two beams by eye. Once the frame is even and level, you can begin adding soil to the bed.

Building the beds with 2x6s and 4x4 corner posts requires a little more work. As with the beam method, begin by laying out the bed location with string or chalk. Then work with the children to measure these distances and transfer the dimensions to the 2x6 boards using a pencil.

If your children are skilled enough to use a handsaw, have them cut each board to length. If the children are not skilled enough, you'll have to cut the boards to length yourself or design the beds to accommodate the length of the boards, as I discussed previously. If the bed is only going to be 6 in. high, you

may not need to reinforce the corners with 4x4 posts. If this is the case, have the children nail the boards together at each end with two or three 16d galvanized nails (which resist rusting).

If you need to reinforce the corners with 4x4 posts, now's the time to cut them to length. The length of the posts will depend on the height of your bed. In general, the posts should extend above the stacked 2x6 boards by about 7½ in. Give the children some hammers and have them attach the 2x6s to each corner post with two 16d galvanized nails, one board at a time, as shown in the drawing on p. 39. Next, have the children sand the edges of the frame corners with rough sandpaper (80-grit should do) to avoid splinters in little hands and knees. I avoided this step once, and the stories still haunt me.

When the frame has been nailed together, gather the family together (or whoever's involved in the garden) to carry it to its location in the garden. Now you're ready to add the soil and begin planting.

CHAPTER FOUR

Preparing the Soil Organically

To a child, preparing the soil of a garden bed is just like playing.

Once the garden area has been laid out or raised beds have been built, the next step is for you and your children to prepare the soil. Soil supplies nutrients to the crops to promote steady and rapid plant growth and acts as the medium of support for plant roots. Well-prepared, high-quality soil can help ensure a successful growing season, allowing the children to reap the true fruits of their labor quickly. I think the best and most healthy method of preparing the soil is to take an organic approach. That means no man-made chemicals, just natural fertilizers.

In this chapter I'll discuss the benefits of gardening organically. I'll also show you some fun ways to introduce your children to the basics of soil composition and soil preparation. You'll find that there are many things to teach children about the soil in the garden, and there are many ways to make it fun. Let's get dirty!

The Organic Approach to Gardening

Most of us, as parents, try our best to be appropriate role models for our children. The phrase "appropriate role model" is so common in my household that my husband's attempt to hang a spoon from his nose in the middle of dinner often brings cries of, "Mom, Dad's not being an appropriate role model again." Gardening organically with your children is all about being an appropriate role model. It's about ensuring a solid future for your family; producing healthy, wholesome, flavorful vegetables; having respect for the earth; and making recycling part of daily gardening activities as well as your daily life.

Why I garden organically

Several years ago, I had a gardening experience that sealed forever my choice to be an organic gardener. A month into the growing season, I noticed an onslaught of striped cucumber beetles. The tiny pests were everywhere, devouring cucumber plants, radishes, and other tasty treats in the south end of my garden. I began picking the demons off, one by one, in an attempt to salvage my crop of slicing cucumbers. At times I felt I had conquered the beetles, but they always returned with a vengeance. There were simply too many to remove by hand.

For the first (and only) time in my gardening life, I purchased a chemical pesticide from the local garden store—some evil powder with warnings up and down the sides of the canister. Now, I have the benefit of master gardener training (for more on the master gardener program, see the sidebar at right) and know how to use pesticides safely. But I still had concerns about the safety of the product and about whether the vegetables would be

okay for my family to eat. So I consulted the manager of the store where I purchased the powder, and he warned me not to eat the tiny cucumbers that already had formed because the pesticide would coat the fruit and would be difficult to wash off. He assured me, however, that the new fruit would be fine.

ASK A MASTER GARDENER

A master gardener is a great gardening resource for you and your children. In states where the program exists, master gardeners are volunteers trained by the state Cooperative Extension Service to provide horticultural information to home gardeners.

Master gardeners are trained in various aspects of horticulture, from botany and soil science to entomology and pesticide safety. The master gardener program was created in 1972 by Washington's Cooperative Extension Service. The program has since spread to 48 states.

For a master gardener, gardening is typically a lifelong passion, and it may even be a person's career, whether working at a nursery, as a landscaper, or as a farmer. Most master gardeners volunteer about 40 hours each year to giving gardening advice to the public.

Many master gardeners enjoy working with children. So it might be worthwhile to invite a master gardener to your home (or your children's school) once you have received your soil-test results. A master gardener can help explain the results to the children and provide you with a lot of information about the soil amendments that may be called for. The person can also be a great source for other gardening information.

I sprinkled the powder over and around the cucumber plants, and the bugs died instantly, never to reappear. I picked the existing cucumbers and tossed them into the trash as the store manager recommended. (I remember feeling sad about this, as the first fruit had been picture-perfect.)

A week or so later, new cucumbers began to grow. The plants looked vigorous and healthy, and the weather that particular summer was perfect for crops of any type. However, the new fruit of the cucumber plants that had been powdered were grotesquely malformed, with multiple cucumbers hooked together as one piece of fruit. The cucumbers were stunted, rotted easily, and were either completely tasteless or so bitter that they were inedible. I was so horrified that I threw away the picked cucumbers, ripped all

of the remaining plants out, and let the bed rest until the following year.

I had learned my lesson. If the pesticide had found its way into the plants so quickly as to completely mutate the new fruit, what could it do to my young children's bodies? I simply was not willing to find out. As a parent, I had to respect the fragility of my children's health. Which is why, since that summer so many years ago, I have become—exclusively—an organic gardener, growing produce without pesticides and chemical enhancements. If problems occur that I can't overcome organically, I consult with various local organic farmers and gardener associations to get some help (I'll talk more about organic pest control in Chapter 6).

Why organic gardening is important to all of us

When you garden organically, you make an impact greater than just good-tasting food and the ability to eat what you have produced without fear of physical side effects. Organic gardening and farming methods affect our health, economic systems, and environment. Talk to your children about these issues during a family meeting. Their wonderful, innocent insight into the state of our earth and their future can make these discussions about gardening quite lively and intriguing.

Get your children to think about the impact their gardening choices can have on the earth and how those choices can affect the health of future generations. Introduce the subject of

Because I garden organically, I don't worry about my children eating fruits or veggies straight from the garden.

self-sustaining lifestyles, so important to developing countries, and talk about the costs of pesticides and chemical fertilizers and how they compare to using the elements naturally found in the gardener's environment. In recent years, there has been an impressive rise in the availability of thoroughly natural products for gardeners, which has resulted in more and more gardeners reaching for natural amendments (or improvements), such as seaweed, peat moss, fish emulsion, bonemeal, compost, and manure, rather than chemicals that guarantee gargantuan vegetables overnight. These organic amendments tend to cost less than most chemical amendments.

What's more, these materials are typically made from recycled, natural materials (bonemeal and compost), are by-products of animals (fish emulsion and manure), or are natural materials (seaweed and peat moss). By using organic materials in your garden, you are helping to keep the environment clean and uncluttered.

These factors all steered me toward organic gardening, but the best reason of all for growing an organic garden is that I have no qualms about my children picking fruit or vegetables and popping them right into their mouths.

To begin an organic family garden, agree with your children to a few simple rules:

- Improve the garden soil with only organic matter and fertilizers.
- Do not use pesticides, fungicides, or herbicides.
- Do not use chemical fertilizers.

Organic gardening depends on natural and noninvasive methods of tending your plantings. They key to gardening successfully in this manner is healthy soil. Many organic gardeners and farmers believe if they feed the soil, the soil will, in turn, feed the plants. To create and maintain healthy soil, you and your children must next understand the basics of soil science.

Soil Basics for Children

After a long winter, it won't take much prodding to convince your children to get outside and start digging in the garden. Children and soil mix effortlessly. Perhaps it is the innate desire of virtually all children to get dirty—really dirty—at any opportunity or the fact that the soil is just there, waiting to be dug, patted, sifted, and shoveled (and sometimes thrown!).

As parents, we often forget the real science involved in preparing the garden as we test the soil, decide how to enrich it, and then measure out the soil amendments. Imagine the look of amazement on your children's faces when they are asked to don lab gloves and prepare test tubes of soil, mixing solutions and analyzing results to determine the soil's nutrient composition.

To prepare for your backyard laboratory, you need to teach your children about when to work the soil, soil types, and the chemical composition of soil.

compost, peat moss, and manure (for more on working amendments into the soil, see pp. 59-60).

Peat-type soil is darker than most other soils, appearing very dark brown to almost black. When the children squeeze it, they'll say it feels like peat moss, foam, or shredded paper. This soil type tends to be very rich in organic matter, but it absorbs moisture too readily, resulting in a garden that promotes root decay rather than root growth. To create proper drainage and airflow in this soil type, have the children add gravel or loam.

Sandy-type soil is easily recognizable. When squeezed, it may not hold any shape at all and, it if does, crumbles instantly after formed. Water, air, and soluble nutrients can quickly flow through sandy-type soil, and it dries out and warms up easily. Because water and nutrients often leach out quickly, sandy-type soil is not very fertile, requiring a lot of amendments if you are to have a successful garden. The children should work manure in deeply and add plenty of peat moss, compost, and/or sawdust to the top layer of the soil to help create a fertile topsoil.

Loam-type soil is what you and your children should hope to have, as it contains a balanced mixture of various sized crumbs of organic matter and soil particles. If the children can squeeze a handful of soil into a ball that falls apart easily, you more than likely are lucky enough to have loam-type soil. Though "ideal," loam-type soil needs some help in maintaining fertility and good structure. Have the children work in organic matter such as compost and manure.

Finding the soil's chemical composition

Along with knowing your soil type, it's also important for you and your children to learn about the chemical composition of the soil so that they are well prepared to manage the mineral nutrition of their growing plants. The best way to discover the chemical composition of the soil is to conduct a soil test.

Because soil can change as new materials are added and plants, insects, worms, and rodents remove and release nutrients, it is a very good idea for the children to test the soil at least every other year. If they (and you) are creating a garden for the first time, testing, in my mind, is not just advisable but necessary.

Soil testing can be done with a home test kit, and children will have fun using it. But this type of test is not 100% accurate, and the results should be viewed as rough estimates of the actual levels of available nutrients in the soil. For a minimal charge ($5 to $10 per test), you can have a much more accurate test performed by the laboratory of your state's Cooperative Extension Service. The service will supply you with a sealable container for the soil sample and a questionnaire, which you fill out so that the laboratory knows your planting preferences and garden location.

The children should send in a sample from each individual bed they are filling with plantings, as soil composition can vary drastically, even though the beds may only be a few feet apart. To take a soil sample, have the children use a very clean trowel or spade and dig down to root depth, usually 6 in. to 8 in., and put the sample in a clean bucket. (The tools should be cleaned with a solution of hot water and 10% bleach.) For an accurate reading of the entire bed, the children should take samples from a number of areas in the same bed and mix them together in the bucket. After mixing, have them take a sample from the bucket, put it in the lab container, seal it, and then send it out. Results are often mailed back within two or three weeks from the date you ship the sample.

The extension-service laboratory will send you a written explanation of the results. You and your children will learn what nutrients are present in the soil, the pH of the soil, as well as what, if any, contaminants are present. You may also learn what needs to be added to your soil to improve it and other tips for growing your crops.

Nutrient levels

The amount and balance of nutrients in the soil has an effect on plant growth. Low levels of nutrients slow

A home test kit is a fun way for children to begin learning about the chemical composition of the garden soil.

plant growth while high levels can pollute the environment or cause imbalances. The results of the soil test let the children know if they need to add more nutrients and how much, helping the children achieve their real goal: great vegetables ready to eat in as short a time as possible.

Plants need a variety of nutrients for survival, including calcium, magnesium, sulfur, iron, manganese, zinc, copper, molybdenum, and boron. But the three major plant foods necessary for successful growth are nitrogen (N), phosphorus (P), and potassium (K). A healthy balance of these three nutrients is a ratio of between 1-2-1 to 4-6-3.

Nitrogen is required for all phases of a plant's growth and development. Too much nitrogen causes leaves and shoots to grow excessively, while a deficiency causes the plant to be stunted. Blood meal, manure, cottonseed meal, and compost, when added to the soil, increase the nitrogen level.

Phosphorus is responsible for efficient and quick maturity, strong stems, resistance to disease, and the flowering, fruiting, and root branching of the plant. A deficiency of phosphorus will result in plants that will flower but not fruit. To increase the level of phosphorus, have the children add bonemeal or fish meal.

Potassium is critical to the formation of sugars and starches, directly affecting the flavor and color of the plant. A potassium deficiency can lead to small or misshapen fruit, as well as to an underdeveloped root system. Low levels can be corrected by adding manure, seaweed, wood ash, or granite dust to your soil.

pH level

The pH of the soil is a measurement of relative acidity or alkalinity based on a scale of 0 to 14, with 0 being acidic, 7 being balanced, and 14 being alkaline (see the chart on the facing page). The pH results of the soil test are important because an imbalance in the pH can result in the loss of valuable nutrients. On average, most vegetable crops enjoy a pH of between 6.0 to 6.8, but you and your children should consult the seed packets or catalogs to be sure of the correct pH level for your plants.

Soil that is too acidic is not suitable for most plants. In very acidic soil—pH below 5.5—phosphorus becomes unavailable to plants, and such nutrients as calcium, magnesium, and potassium have an increased tendency to leach out of the soil. (A calcium deficiency will cause buds and young leaves to die back at their tips, and a deficiency of magnesium will result in the stunted growth of the plant.) In addition, beneficial soil bacteria begin to slow their work of turning organic matter into humus, which will adversely affect the structure of the soil.

Also, very acidic soil can cause earthworms to move out of your garden to a more palatable patch of soil. You do not want a mass exodus of

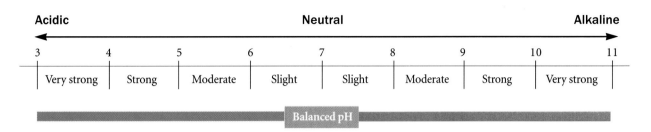

Acidic   **Neutral**   **Alkaline**

3	4	5	6	7	8	9	10	11
Very strong	Strong	Moderate	Slight	Slight	Moderate	Strong	Very strong	

Balanced pH

Add natural limestone, bonemeal, wood ash, pulverized eggshells, clamshells, or oyster shells.

Add pine needles, cottonseed meal, leaf mold, peat moss, wood chips, or sawdust.

earthworms if you are to have a healthy garden, as earthworms contribute organic matter and tiny tunnels that help air and moisture move through the soil. To help acidic soil become more balanced, add lime or natural amendments with high levels of lime, such as bonemeal, wood ash, pulverized eggshells, clamshells, or oyster shells.

A very high alkaline level—a pH above 7.5—causes certain nutrients necessary for healthy plant growth to be unavailable. Also, in very alkaline soil, humus breaks apart, causing organic matter to be ineffective, and salts may become concentrated, which could be toxic to certain plants. If your pH tests show that the soil is too alkaline, have the children add to the soil sulfur or amendments with high levels of sulfur, such as pine needles, cottonseed meal, leaf mold, peat moss, wood chips, or sawdust.

Contaminants

As healthy as the soil may look, it could be housing abnormally high metal or chemical levels that might be a health hazard. Remember, as I mentioned when talking about treated lumber (see Chapter 3), fruit and vegetables will take in whatever is in the soil, so it is wise to test and learn what minerals or chemicals might be present in your soil.

If you are gardening near a new construction site, where fuels may spill from heavy machinery, or near an older public facility, such as a school or church that may have been built before the harms of lead were recognized, you may want to have the chemical composition of the soil tested. The Cooperative Extension Service laboratory will test for lead and other metal contamination, and some laboratories test for other detectable chemicals, such as arsenic. If your results indicate unhealthy levels of either metal or chemicals, ask the extension service for advice on how to correct the problem. Another great source for help in understanding the soil-test results is a master gardener (see the sidebar on p. 43).

Soil Preparation

How you treat your soil is the most important facet of organic gardening for your children to learn. The foundation of organic gardening rests upon improving, or amending, the garden soil with matter that is generally defined as organic. There are two basic methods that an organic gardener can use to prepare the soil for planting: adding compost and working it into the soil or adding organic fertilizers.

Composting doesn't require a lot of space. These two 4-ft. square bins provide my family with enough black gold to last the season.

Composting for the young

There are many types of organic soil amendments: animal manures (fresh manure contains high levels of ammonia, which will kill plants, so be sure to let it decompose before adding it to your garden); mulches of leaves, straw, and hay; and green manure crops, such as red clover and winter rye, which are planted simply to be turned back into the ground. But no better amendment exists than compost. Compost is chemically balanced—typically with a pH of around 7—so it won't alter the existing pH of the soil, retains nutrients, and is the one soil amendment that can turn both hopelessly dense clay soil or loose sandy soil into rich, fertile loam.

Compost is created by combining organic waste materials under controlled conditions so that the ingredients decompose and eventually become humus—dark-colored, forest-smelling matter rich in nutrients. Now stop and think about this idea, and you will realize why children and composting are a natural match. Composting relies upon waste as the primary ingredient. Who can possibly produce more waste per body pound than children? When composting, children make a pile of disgusting stuff, use a pitchfork to play with it, and, finally, dig up shovelfuls of stuff that smells like the deep woods right after a rain and helps their plants grow like gangbusters. What's more, composting is easy. Here's how it works.

The science of composting

Your goal in building a compost pile is to provide the best possible conditions for the decomposition of organic matter. Organisms in the compost pile critical to the decomposition process ask only for the basics of life: a balanced diet, water, air, and warmth. It is very easy for you and your children to provide these simple basics.

Compost organisms require a balanced diet of carbon (for energy) and nitrogen (for forming protein). This balance, often referred to as the C/N ratio, has a direct effect on the rate of decomposition. For instance, if there is not enough nitrogen or there is excess carbon in the compost pile, decomposition will be slowed and nitrogen will be depleted. If too much nitrogen and not enough carbon exists, nitrogen is wasted as it escapes into the air, causing unpleasant odors, or into the ground water, creating pollution problems.

The ideal C/N ratio is 25-30:1. When this ideal C/N ratio is maintained, and with the proper amount of moisture and airflow, the organisms in the pile actively feed and help the materials decompose. In turn, the energy provided by this feeding process creates enough heat in the pile (as high as 150°F) to kill off any harmful bacteria or organisms. How your pile functions is all a matter of what you and your children put into it and how it is distributed.

Adding the right stuff

To begin composting, you have to collect the right organic matter so that you can maintain the ideal C/N ratio. That means you and your children should alternate the pile with high-carbon matter, such as sawdust, pine needles, leaves, and straw, and high-nitrogen materials, such as grass clippings, table scraps, fruit waste, and weeds.

As a general description, let your children know that high-carbon materials are usually brown or yellow, dry, and bulky, while high-nitrogen matter tends to be green, moist, and often sloppy. To ensure that the organisms you need to do the work

Sawdust, pine needles, dried leaves, and shredded paper supply much-needed carbon to the organisms in the compost pile. (Photo by Susan Kahn.)

Eggshells, vegetable and fruit scraps, and grass clippings bring nitrogen to the composting mix. (Photo by Susan Kahn.)

down very slowly and will, sure as you can bet, attract animals to the composter. Also, steer away from industrial waste products, such as that generated by paper mills, which often sell pulp by-products as mulches. These by-products often contain chemicals or bleach. And do not—under any circumstances—put diseased plants or plants treated with chemical pesticides into your compost pile. The pile may not heat up enough to kill the diseases, and the chemicals may remain throughout the composting process. The resulting compost will help you spread the disease or chemicals to your garden.

Buying or building a compost bin

Now that you and your children know what to put into a compost pile, you need a place to compost. Fortunately, you do not need a huge space. One 3-ft.-square space will provide a gardener with enough "black gold" for the season. Nowadays you can buy a commercial compost tumbler, or you and your children can make a simple composting bin right in your backyard.

A commercial compost tumbler, also known as a barrel or drum composter, can be purchased at your local garden center or hardware store. A compost tumbler allows you to compost with little physical labor. You don't have to turn the pile with a pitchfork or shovel—you simply crank a handle on the tumbler to turn it round and round. The tumbler can also produce compost quickly—in as little as two to three weeks. However, a compost tumbler has a very limited capacity, and

are present, toss in some rich garden soil or, better yet, finished compost. Other materials that are welcome additions to a compost pile are eggshells, coffee grounds, chicken manure, wood ash from woodstoves or fireplaces, wood chips, and sawdust (just be sure the wood has not been treated with chemicals).

Although most any natural material that will break down is okay to put into a compost pile, there are some materials to avoid. Human and pet feces often carry disease organisms, and meat scraps and fatty materials break you have to wait until the compost is "cooked" (finished) to start a new batch. (Gardeners I know who use compost tumblers still gather materials to be composted, but instead of putting them right into the tumbler, they store them in a plastic tub with a tight-fitting lid until the batch in the tumbler is cooked. To absorb odors, they sprinkle sawdust in the plastic tub.)

Making a compost bin, however, can be a fun project for the whole family, and it doesn't have to be complicated. For instance, you and the children can make a small one from a plastic garbage can. Simply cut off the bottom of the can and punch holes through the sides to provide air circulation. Then it's a simple matter of putting the composter in a convenient location and adding the appropriate materials. This simple composter can provide rich compost in about six months.

Another option is for you and the children to build a compost bin out of 2x lumber and wire fencing (see the sidebar on pp. 56-57). This two-bin composter has worked well for me. It has wide openings in front, so shoveling in materials and turning the pile are easy. The wire mesh around the bins allows moisture and air to penetrate. And best of all, the materials to build it are relatively inexpensive, and the project takes *maybe* 1½ hours to construct. The two-bin composter allows me to work two piles at once. Typically I have one pile that's being added to and worked, with the other pile consisting of finished compost. My family can produce a batch of compost in about six weeks in these two bins.

A compost pile must be turned frequently to help the materials decompose.

Maintaining the compost pile

Nature does most of the composting work. But there are a few things you and the children will have to do to ensure efficient decomposition. You must turn the pile frequently, keep the size of the pile manageable, and make sure the pile has adequate moisture.

Turning the compost pile provides adequate aeration, moisture distribution, and efficient decomposition. For a hot and quick compost pile, frequent turning means every few days.

As I mentioned on p. 53, the heat produced by the process of decay is key to making compost. To maintain the proper heat, make sure you and the children keep the pile at a minimum of 3 ft. square. A pile smaller than that will not heat up adequately to decompose

Materials
- Thirteen 8-ft. 2x4s (use nonleaching pressure-treated wood)
- Six $3/8$-in. by 6-in. carriage bolts (with nuts and washers)
- Four $3/8$-in. by 4-in. carriage bolts
- One 20-ft. by 4-ft. piece galvanized wire mesh
- About 50 16d galvanized nails
- One box $3/4$-in. galvanized staples

This two-bin composter can be a fun project for you and your children, and it won't take all day to build. Follow these instructions, and refer to the drawing and materials list for more information.

Begin with the three 4-ft. by 4-ft. panels (the middle and side panels). Cut six 8-ft. 2x4s to 4 ft. long. For each panel, nail four 2x4 pieces together with 16d galvanized nails (which resist rust). Two nails should be sufficient at each joint.

Using wire cutters, cut three pieces of the wire mesh (available at most hardware stores) to 4 ft. by 4 ft. and staple one piece to each panel using $3/4$-in. staples. Both the mesh and staples should be galvanized to resist rust.

To build the back panel, cut three 8-ft. 2x4s to 4 ft. and attach them to two 8-ft. 2x4s with 16d nails (again, two at each joint should be all that's needed). Then staple the 4-ft. by 8-ft. piece of mesh to the panel.

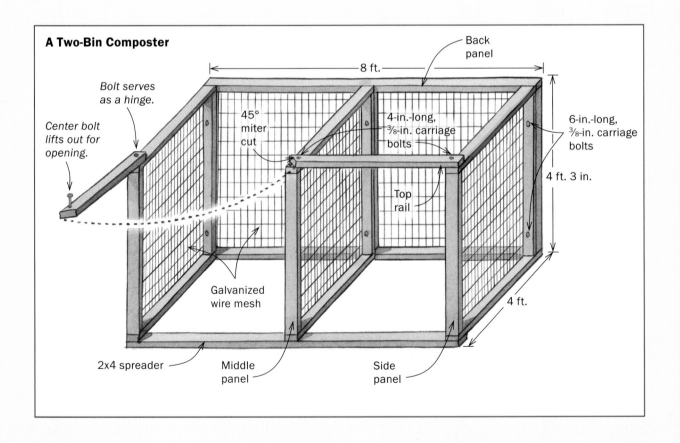

A Two-Bin Composter

Bolt serves as a hinge.

Center bolt lifts out for opening.

Back panel

8 ft.

45° miter cut

4-in.-long, $3/8$-in. carriage bolts

6-in.-long, $3/8$-in. carriage bolts

4 ft. 3 in.

Top rail

Galvanized wire mesh

4 ft.

2x4 spreader

Middle panel

Side panel

Now attach the 4-ft. by 4-ft. panels to the back panel. Start with the middle panel. Align it with the center 2x4 of the back panel, drill two ⅜-in. holes through the adjoining members, and attach them with two 6-in.-long, ⅜-in. carriage bolts. Repeat for the side panels.

Now install the 8-ft. 2x4 spreader on the bottom of the front of the bin, which helps reinforce the side panels against the outward push of the compost pile. Attach the spreader to each small panel with two 16d nails.

The last step is to attach two 4-ft. 2x4 rails to the front of the bin. These rails also help reinforce the bin. Miter-cut an 8-ft. 2x4 at the 4-ft. mark. (A miter cut is a 45° cut, but you don't have to be exact here, just close enough that the two pieces will fit together.) Then place one rail on top of the bin and drill two ⅜-in. holes through it and the adjoining members (be sure to drill around any nails). Repeat for the other rail.

Now slip a 4-in.-long, ⅜-in. carriage bolt into each hole. The bolts on the outside ends of the rails will serve as hinges, while the ones in the center can be removed so you can open the rails to add to or turn the compost pile.

My son Bennett and his friend Jasper screen a batch of compost before adding it to the garden.

the materials. You also have to be sure the pile doesn't get too big. A pile that is too large cannot be turned easily, so aeration and moisture distribution will not be effective, resulting in a pile that does not heat up sufficiently for quick decomposition. If you add the right materials and keep the pile to about 5 ft. high, your compost will heat up even in fall and winter. The steam that escapes when the pile is turned during the cold weather never ceases to widen my eyes, and the children love to warm their hands over the pile. When there's heat, there's compost on the way.

Moisture is a necessary ingredient for the decomposition process. Often the materials you add (the green stuff, in particular) provide sufficient moisture. But if you are in a dry climate or are having a drier-than-normal season, you may need to water the compost once in a while or as you add materials to it.

Screening compost

The compost is ready to use when it is crumbly, dark brown, and uniform in texture. It will possess a smell reminiscent of the woods after a warm summer rain. I think it smells great. My children think I'm gross but agree that it doesn't smell like rotted garbage, contains no bizarre worms or other disgusting bugs, and smells like the woods. But don't expect perfection. Some things decompose slower than others, and you are bound to wind up with items in the compost pile that haven't broken down, such as large sticks. Also, there may be items that got into the pile that won't break down at all, such as rocks, wire twist ties, and maybe even an ice-cream wrapper or two. It's important to rid the compost of these materials, or they may interfere with root development.

To rid the compost of any unwanted material, make some compost screens so that the children can sift out the bad stuff. All you need are four 3-ft. strips of wood (about 1 in. by 1 in.), one 3-ft. square piece of ¼-in. screening, a staple gun, and ¾-in. staples. Have the children attach the four strips of wood with staples (see the drawing below) to make a frame. Then have the children staple the screening to the frame.

To screen the compost, put a shovelful of finished compost on the screen and shake it over a wheelbarrow,

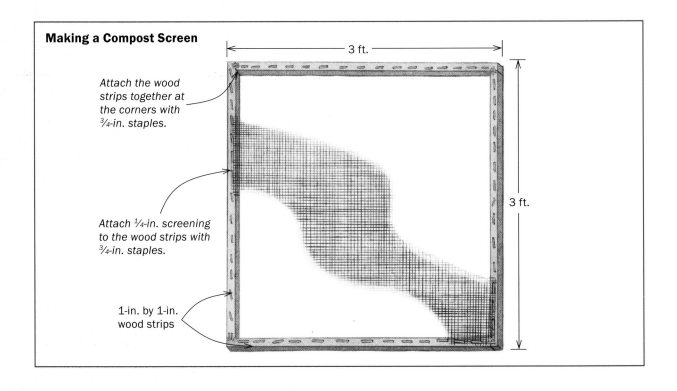

Making a Compost Screen

3 ft.

Attach the wood strips together at the corners with ¾-in. staples.

Attach ¼-in. screening to the wood strips with ¾-in. staples.

1-in. by 1-in. wood strips

3 ft.

allowing the good compost to fall in the wheelbarrow and larger remnants to remain on top of the screen. Throw any compostable leftovers back into the pile that's cooking, and toss away anything that will not decompose, such as rocks or wire twist ties. This way, nothing that can be composted goes to waste.

Other sources of compost

If you are not able to begin a compost pile in time to amend your garden in spring or fall, search out other sources of this gardener's black gold. Many towns run composting projects and offer compost to residents at no charge. If you take advantage of such a resource, remember to screen the compost before using it. Large composting efforts such as these will not have been screened for large materials. You may also find compost at farms, nurseries, or landscape companies that may have extra.

Adding compost to the beds

Once you and your children have a supply of compost, and after it has been screened, it's time to add it to the beds. Before doing so, however, you and the children should double dig the beds so that the soil is loose and aerated, promoting healthy plant growth. Double digging requires a bit of work from most of the children and adults involved in the garden (see the drawing at right).

Starting at one end of the bed, dig a trench about 1 ft. deep and place the soil in a wheelbarrow. Loosen the remaining subsoil in the trench with a

Double Digging Beds

Loosened subsoil

Step 1. Dig a 1-ft.-deep trench, place the soil in a wheelbarrow, and loosen the subsoil in the trench with a pitchfork.

Step 2. Dig a trench next to the first and place this soil in the first. Loosen the subsoil in the second trench with a pitchfork. Repeat across the entire bed.

Step 3. Place the soil from the wheelbarrow into the last trench. Then spread a 3-in. layer of compost or other amendment across the entire bed to create a fertile topsoil.

After double digging the bed (see p. 59) to aerate and loosen the existing soil, pour the compost into the bed (top) and then spread it around, creating a 3-in. layer of fertile topsoil (bottom).

pitchfork. Then dig a trench next to the first one—the same depth—and place the soil from the second trench into the first. Again, loosen the soil at the bottom of the second trench with a pitchfork. Repeat the process all the way across the bed. Fill the last trench in the bed with the soil from the first trench (in the wheelbarrow). When you are done, spread the compost on the bed to a minimum depth of 3 in. (you can add more if you prefer).

This part of your gardening project will be the most labor intensive, so be sure to invite all to participate, but don't force the smaller or younger children to keep up the digging too long. The last thing you want is for the children to be so sore that they choose not to continue gardening after the digging. Take the time to explain to your crew why double digging makes such a difference to the end product so that they don't feel they are working hard for nothing.

Fertilizing

Another method of adding nutrients to the soil is to use organic fertilizers. Organic gardens rarely require these fertilizers since organically managed soil, rich with compost, is biologically active and rich in nutrients. However, many organic gardeners use fertilizers as gourmet cooks use herbs: to add the finishing touch that brings out the very best in plants.

It is important to help your children understand the close association in organic gardening between fertilizers and soil conditions and to use only organic fertilizers. Chemical fertilizers contain mineral salts that are readily available for uptake by plant roots. However, these salts do not contain organic matter that can act as a source of food for earthworms and microorganisms. These fertilizers often repel earthworms because they increase the acidity of the soil. If chemical fertilizers are continually introduced to the soil, the organic structure of that soil will break down and beneficial microorganisms will all but disappear. More and more chemicals will be needed to feed the plants because the organic plant food contained in all soil will have been depleted.

Natural additives and techniques

If necessary, you and your children can choose to custom-fertilize each plant according to that plant's needs or use a mixed organic fertilizer that is good throughout the garden for all plants.

If you fertilize individual plants, you and the children will need to decide exactly what that plant needs based on the soil-test results. After having the children examine the soil-test results,

have them analyze the plant itself, either from planting information if you are just transplanting, or from observation of the plant in the garden. Have the children determine what the plant is lacking, and therefore what fertilizer is needed and the correct amount.

Should you and your children decide to fertilize the whole garden, there are several organic fertilizers available on the market in both dry and liquid form. Dry fertilizers are easy to make on your own, as long as you blend the ingredients to achieve a balanced N-P-K ratio between 1-2-1 and 4-6-3 (see p. 50 for more on soil nutrients). Using the chart below, choose one organic ingredient from each column and mix them together. Regardless of the material, the mix will give you a balanced N-P-K ratio and will bring to your garden an even supply of nutrients that will encourage your plants to thrive.

There are also several liquid fertilizers available for your garden, the most common organic ones being

ACHIEVING A BALANCED N-P-K RATIO

Nitrogen (N)	Phosphorus (P)	Potassium (K)
2 parts blood meal	6 parts rock phosphate	6 parts greensand
3 parts fish meal	3 parts bonemeal	1 part kelp meal

Choose one natural ingredient from each column and mix them together according to the recommended amounts to achieve a balanced N-P-K ratio between 1-2-1 and 4-6-3.

Seaweed is a good source of nutrients. Just be sure to rinse it well and work it into the soil; otherwise, it may give off an unpleasant odor.

fish or seaweed by-products. You can also make your own "fertilizer tea" by brewing some compost in water until it is a weak tea color. Either mix the compost and water and then strain it, or place the compost in a cloth bag and steep it like a tea bag for a couple of days.

Whatever liquid fertilizer you use, it can be broadcast to your entire garden by means of a watering can or a spray bottle. Have the children spray the garden either in the early morning (before school or sports camp) or early evening (before baths, homework, or cartoons) when the sun won't dry up the liquid, and the plants can absorb the nutrients quickly. Also, choose a day without rain in the forecast and neither unseasonably cold

nor drastically hot temperatures. The children should spray until the liquid drips off the leaves and then move to the next set of plants.

If you have the good fortune to live near the ocean or will be visiting it during the growing season, harvest some seaweed with your children, if permitted (seaweed is free for the taking in many areas). Seaweed is a perfect garden fertilizer. It will decompose quickly and will provide a good amount of nutrients to your plants. Just be sure to rinse it well before placing it in the garden or compost pile and work it into the soil; otherwise, your backyard could start to smell like a fishing boat.

CHAPTER FIVE

Planting the Garden

Children are often amazed at their success in growing from seed.

When beginning to plant the garden, you and your children enter the phase of gardening where the interests of children and adults may vary greatly. While children seem to love filling containers with soil and planting seeds (or planting seeds directly into the garden), many don't have a lot of patience and may not enjoy waiting for seedlings to grow. Others simply may not be intrigued by the maintenance involved in the process.

In this chapter I'll discuss how to start seeds indoors and outdoors and transplant the new seedlings to the garden, offering suggestions throughout on helping your children develop and maintain their interest in the process. Be aware, however, that the instructions in this chapter are general. For specific planting information (such

When the children start seeds indoors, they'll have healthy seedlings in a short period of time.

as when to start seeds and when to transplant them), consult your seed packets or catalogs.

Starting Seeds Indoors

I suggest you and the children start the majority of crops indoors, where the tender seedlings are protected from wind, cold, drought, disease, insects, and animals (if you have cats or rabbits in the house, be sure to keep them away from the seedlings). When starting seeds indoors, you and the children will be able to control the early days of your plants—a critical time for any plant. With a lot of care, the children will grow healthy seedlings in a short period of time, ensuring that their efforts have been worthwhile. Growing

healthy seedlings means you and your family will enjoy a hardy garden and bountiful harvest.

Working with soilless growing medium

The easiest way to start seeds indoors is to begin with soilless growing medium. Unlike soil from the backyard, soilless growing medium will be sterile, meaning it's free of weeds, diseases, and insects. Soilless growing medium also holds moisture and nutrients longer than backyard soil, allowing these things to be released evenly to the plants over time. Although soilless growing medium holds moisture and nutrients for a long time, it is not dense, allowing air to circulate, and doesn't create mud, which makes cleanup easy. Soilless growing medium typically contains a mixture of peat moss, vermiculite, and various nutrients and is available at most garden centers and nurseries.

Because soilless growing medium can be very dry, water it down while it is still in the bag and then transfer it to the containers while still wet. This way the children will not be engulfed in clouds of dust as they try to transfer the growing medium to the containers. The children will be amazed at how much water the bag of medium can absorb, so let them loose with a spray bottle or watering can until all the medium in the bag is moist but not dripping.

Adding growing medium to the containers

Once the growing medium has been moistened, it's time for the children to get their hands dirty and place it into

FUN METHODS OF STARTING SEEDS

There are a couple of alternate ways to germinate seeds that children often find fun and that actually may speed germination. The first involves making a "honey disk" and the other is the "brick-is-alive" method.

Making a honey disk requires some two-ply tissue, some honey (or corn or maple syrup), soilless growing medium, a tray, and the seeds. Fill the tray with moist growing medium. Cut 1-in. squares of two-ply tissue and then separate the plies. Place the single plies into the tray and put two or three dabs of honey on each one. Place one seed on each dab of honey. Then press the second plies over the first ones. When the seedlings come up, the children can transplant them directly to larger containers.

To make a brick come to life, you'll need a standard building brick, a shallow pan, some soilless growing medium, and the seeds. Begin by soaking a brick in water overnight. After soaking, set the brick in the shallow pan and add water until it's about ½ in. from the top of the brick. Spread 1 in. of soilless growing medium on top of the brick and have the children sow the seeds directly into the medium. Water will keep rising through the porous brick through capillary action and will keep the growing medium moist. Maintain the water level and watch the seedlings grow.

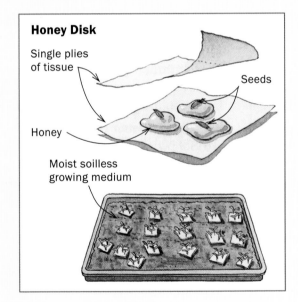

Honey Disk

Single plies of tissue

Seeds

Honey

Moist soilless growing medium

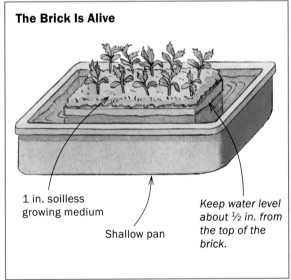

The Brick Is Alive

1 in. soilless growing medium

Shallow pan

Keep water level about ½ in. from the top of the brick.

Although planting seedlings in a garden is easy and often ensures a healthy start to your garden, some plants simply have to be planted directly into the ground. Root vegetables, such as carrots, beets, and parsnips, cannot withstand the shock of being transplanted and have to be started in the ground where they will eventually grow. Other seeds, such as peas and beans, grow very quickly and simply don't need to be started indoors. Cool-weather loving plants, such as lettuce, spinach, arugula, and other greens, often do even better when they are started by direct seeding, particularly if you help their germination along with a floating row cover.

Planting seeds directly into the garden requires no magic wand, no mysterious formula. You and your children need only the knowledge of when to seed, the soil temperature required to germinate particular seeds, and a few simple tools. The plant data sheets the children created while planning the garden (see Chapter 2) will give the children the precise timing for direct seeding of each plant and the soil temperature required.

When the date for direct seeding nears, have the children monitor the soil temperature for a few days. When the optimum seeding temperature has been reached, have the children grab a hand trowel, string, a yardstick, some pencils, and the seed packets. Then the family can head for the garden.

There's no mystery to planting seeds directly into the garden. The children simply need to follow instructions on the seed packets or plant data sheets.

LAYING OUT PLANTING ROWS

I like to plant in rows, unless I am starting plants that require more space or a different planting scheme, such as hills or trellises. The even row of little plants emerging from the soil is really pleasant to the eye, and I believe that children feel more proud and recognize the work they have done when the rows appear with some measure of uniformity. It is also easier to distinguish weeds from plants than it would be if you were simply to sprinkle, or broadcast, seeds over a plot.

To help the children plant in rows, it's a good idea to lay out the rows with string. Have them tie the string (old kite string works fine, or even leftover yarn) onto a pencil and poke the pencil into the ground where they want the row to begin. Have them stretch the string across the garden to the spot that ends the row, tie the string to a second pencil, and stick it into the ground. Another method of achieving straight rows for the children is to place a long garden tool, such as a rake, next to the row they want to plant in and use it as a guide.

PLANTING THE SEEDS

Have the children use a trowel to dig out the row, following the planting depth on their data sheets. Then they can place the seeds in the row according to the spacing requirements for each plant. Encourage the children to seed carefully; otherwise, they may have to do a lot of thinning later on, which is the tedious task of pulling out baby plants from the row to make room for the stronger ones. A yardstick is helpful for judging the spacing of seeds, guaranteeing plenty of growing space. However, if you have young children who may not be able to read a yardstick yet or who don't have fully developed motor skills, help them spread the seeds out so that a whole bunch of seeds won't end up in one 2-in. spot.

Young children may need your help with spacing and planting seeds.

When used in combination with the string guide, the yardstick will also help the children plant in a straight line, resulting in a neat-looking garden. Children will feel a great sense of pride in the tidy row they create.

Once the seeds have been placed, have the children cover them with garden soil or soilless growing medium, pat the soil firmly, and water the seeds lightly with a watering can or hose. My son Seth still calls this task "putting the seeds to bed," because he covers them up, tucks them in, and gives them a pat.

As with indoor planting, watering is important, so set up a watering schedule with the children so that they keep the germinating seeds moist.

Growing new seedlings successfully is a fascinating experience for children.

enough to damage the seedlings and will jar the seedling roots just enough to make it easy to separate the plants.

When separating and transplanting the seedlings, be sure the children pick them up by their leaves, not by the stems. The stem is the most delicate part of the plant and will be crushed upon impact, which will kill the tender seedling.

I recommend waiting a day or two after the true leaves appear to separate and transplant the seedlings, allowing a bit of extra time for the seedlings to gather strength in their stems. Have the children begin by sterilizing the containers, if necessary (see p. 66). Fill each container or cell to the brim with soilless growing medium. Firm the medium, make a small hole in it, and place the roots of the tiny seedling into the hole.

Plant the seedling deep enough that the top of the soil is level to the cotyledons (which are probably shriveled up by now), then firm the soil

gently around the plant. Have the children label each container after transplanting the seedlings. Keep the seedlings in the same well-lighted location, as they will require a minimum of 12 hours of good light.

These young seedlings should be fed initially with a water-soluble organic fertilizer (try a 20-20-20 mixture) diluted to half or one-third strength. Apply this mixture with a watering can. The seedlings should also be watered thoroughly. Again, it's best to bottom water so you or the children do not damage the seedlings (for more on watering, see p. 68). These plants should not have to be repotted again. But to be safe, a few weeks after transplanting, have the children pop the seedlings out of their containers to examine the roots. If the roots have filled up the bottom of the soil, the seedling should be moved to a larger container because, if the roots start to overtake the soil, the seedling's growth will slow or stop.

Hardening off seedlings

Hardening off the seedlings is the process of acclimating them to the harsher outdoor conditions they will endure when transplanted to the garden. A plant rushed into an outdoor setting with sudden temperature fluctuations, wind, and uneven moisture, can die quickly, or struggle so much to survive that its health is permanently impaired. This sounds like a dire situation, and I realize we are talking about plants. But imagine working with four or five children for weeks, researching, selecting, and then starting seedlings, only to have all of the seedlings die when you plant them into the ground.

If your children have grown their own seedlings, they will need to establish a hardening-off schedule that they should adhere to like glue for about 10 days before transplanting the seedlings outside. If you have purchased seedlings from a nursery or farmer, make sure to ask if the seedlings have been hardened off (for more on buying seedlings, see the sidebar on pp. 76 and 77). In most cases, the seedlings you purchase will be ready for the garden, but some growers may tell you to move the plants—particularly warm-weather plants like tomatoes, peppers, and eggplant—in and out a week before planting just to be sure.

A cold frame is the perfect place to harden off seedlings. It is really a simple wood box with a hinged cover made from an old wooden window or a wood frame covered in plastic or clear vinyl. In the cold frame, the seedlings can grow accustomed to the temperature, moisture, and light variations of the outdoor environment. About 2½ weeks

A cold frame is a great place to harden off seedlings to prepare them for outdoor life.

Growing your own seedlings is quite a bit of work, so don't feel guilty if you opt to buy them. Although you can more than likely find suitable seedlings at your local nursery, I prefer to buy them at a farmer's market.

At a farmer's market, you and the children can find a wide variety of seedlings, such as yellow plum tomatoes, Oriental cucumbers, tomatillos, and cinnamon basil. The farmers are also are eager to share their knowledge, engaging the children in discussions on planting and harvesting. I also like the idea of supporting local farmers, considering the number of farmers who are having a difficult time making a living. As always, I urge you to search out the growers who choose to farm without chemical

At a farmer's market, you can get practical gardening advice from the growers.

Even the youngest children will be captivated by the wealth of choices at a farmer's market.

additives and pesticides. This way, you don't have to worry about unwanted poisons getting into your children's bodies.

Regardless of where you and the children shop for seedlings, have them bring their research on the various plants so that they can ask sound questions. Their research and interest will be appreciated and acknowledged by the nursery workers and farmers.

You may need to call ahead to a nursery if you want the children to spend a lot of time with the folks there. If you and the children want to spend time talking to the farmers at a market, be sure to get there early to avoid the crush of people that happens from about 9 A.M. to noon. During those times, the farmers will lose business if they talk to one customer too long.

Check the seedlings carefully, looking for signs of damage from pest infestation or diseases.

CHOOSING THE BEST SEEDLINGS

Shop as early in the season as you can so that you have a good selection of seedlings from which to choose.

Have the children look for healthy foliage and check the undersides of leaves to make sure they are free of insects or larvae. The children should look for young, stocky seedlings, with blemish-free, deep-green leaves (providing they should be green). They should avoid any yellowing, spindly, weak, long-stemmed seedlings with holes and bites taken out of the leaves. The children should also look at the root structure of the seedlings and avoid those that are pot bound, meaning that the plant roots are covering the bottom of the pot and starting to creep out of the drainage holes or up the sides of the container. These seedlings are starved for room and nutrients and will require more care to survive or produce than you may be able to give.

before planting outdoors, begin to harden the seedlings off by reducing the watering schedule. A week before planting, have the children move the seedlings into the cold frame. The cover of the cold frame should be left open on warm days and closed on cool days or at night (when temperatures dip to below 55°F). After a week in the cold frame, the seedlings should be ready for outdoor life.

CHILD-SIZED TOOLS

I have gardened with children for years and watched them struggle to dig with a full-sized trowel or shovel and clunk themselves on the head with an adult-sized rake or hoe. Because of their difficulty in handling these large tools, the children can get frustrated quickly. One of the tricks to helping make the transplanting task as enjoyable as possible for younger children is to have them working with garden tools that are appropriately sized for their young limbs.

Child-sized tools make gardening easy and fun for small hands.

Many department stores sell plastic gardening toys, which are fine for toddlers who want to pretend they are gardening with dad or mom. However, if you are actually working with preschoolers through grade-schoolers in a vegetable garden, visit your nursery center or peruse your gardening catalogs for solid, child-sized gardening tools. Brio, the famous maker of wooden railroad sets, produces some fine, brightly colored, sturdy trowels, shovels, garden rakes, and hoes, in addition to a small, functional wheelbarrow. These small tools will be a worthwhile investment if you intend to garden with children for more than a year or two. The tools are available at some high-end toy stores and through mail-order sources, such as Johnny's catalog and Shepherd's Seeds catalog.

If you do not have a cold frame, you will have to work with the children to expose the seedlings to the outdoors gradually by moving them in and out of the house. As with the cold-frame method of hardening off, reduce watering about two-and-a-half weeks before planting outdoors. Seven to 10 days before planting, have the children introduce the seedlings to the outdoors by placing them in a protected setting, away from direct wind and sun, for about one hour. After the first day, have the children water the plants well and fertilize them once. Thereafter, have the children increase the seedlings' time outdoors by an hour each day, gradually moving the plants into more and more wind and sunlight, until the seedlings are spending the entire day and part of the early evening outside. Once the planting time has arrived, the seedlings should be well prepared to handle the rough outdoor life.

Help your children set up string guidelines to make it easier for them to transplant seedlings in rows.

Transplanting Seedlings into the Garden

Once the seedlings have been hardened off and the garden area has been prepared with organic amendments, you and the children are ready to transplant the seedlings from their containers to the earth. Because the plants are still tender and fragile—even though they've been hardened off— urge the children to handle the seedlings carefully. For the same reason, if possible, choose an overcast day for

the first transplanting adventure to spare the plants from baking in the hot sun on their first day outdoors.

Preparing for transplant

The actual transplanting can be easily handled by children of almost any age. If your children are too small to handle adult-sized tools, try to find child-sized tools (see the sidebar on the facing page). They will need a hand trowel, some string, some pencils (or wood stakes), a yardstick or tape measure, and, of course, the seedlings.

Children may have a lot of questions about transplanting, so be prepared to lend a hand when necessary.

First have the children lay out rows in the garden area (for more on planting in rows, see the sidebar on pp. 72 and 73). Gardening in rows makes maintenance easier (the children can easily tell the weeds from the plants) and it will be easier to space the seedlings appropriately. Have the children tie the string onto a pencil and poke the pencil halfway into the ground where they want the row to begin. Then stretch the string to where the row

ends, tie the string to a pencil, and stick it into the ground. Now the children are ready to plant.

Here's how the children should plant a seedling. Make a hole in the garden with a trowel. Insert the trowel deep enough to accommodate the plant and then twist the trowel back and forth (describe the motion as screwing on a bottle cap). The hole should be big enough to hold the entire root system enclosed in the seedling's container. If

THE MAGIC OF BLACK PLASTIC

Black plastic is an amazing addition to any garden where seedlings are planted. Although it's ugly, resembling a gathering of black trash bags, it certainly changes the nature of gardening.

Since I have been using black plastic, my run-ins with insects, pests, and disease have decreased dramatically. What's more, the children enjoy putting it down and the results it brings. Weeds won't grow because the plastic will not allow light through for them to sprout, and watering won't have to be done as frequently because the plastic will retain moisture.

Black plastic will also keep the soil under it several degrees warmer than the air temperature, allowing roots to grow and flourish. As an added benefit, earthworms will thrive in the black-plastic environment, helping the garden to remain aerated and organically balanced.

Before using black plastic, though, make sure you and the children have prepared the soil well, as described in Chapter 4. The children should also till or rake the soil to remove any large lumps and rocks, which will interfere with the roots of the growing plants and could tear the plastic.

LAYING IT DOWN

Before laying down the plastic, have the children water the garden. The plastic will seal in the moisture already in the garden. Then place the plastic on the garden. Have the children dig a small trench along the length of the plastic, then pull the plastic smooth and taut (don't become too obsessive about wrinkles— they are bound to appear), leaving the sides in the trench. Anchor the sides with soil from the trench.

Encourage the children to let the plastic sit for about three to five days before planting. This allows the soil to warm, the weeds under the plastic to die (if there are any), and the moisture to be distributed evenly. When planting time arrives, the children will be intrigued by the warmth and moisture of the soil under the plastic (weeks later they will be thrilled by the rapid growth and development of their plants).

To plant, have the children cut slits in the plastic, just big enough to slip in the root balls of their seedlings, and then follow the instructions for transplanting seedlings on pp. 80 and 82.

If your children are suspicious about this gardening wonder, help them create a test garden. Suggest they try growing tomato or

Black plastic will help keep plant roots warm and moist. It also reduces weed and pest problems.

peppers in two plots—one with black plastic and the other without—and see which does better. I guarantee that the plot with plastic will produce healthier plants and quicker fruit than the other plot.

Black plastic is sold at garden centers or through many catalogs. It's available in varying widths and thicknesses, but I suggest purchasing the thickest type you can because it will stand up better over the season.

After the seedlings are in the ground, water them in thoroughly.

the hole is too small, the roots will become overcrowded and will struggle for water.

Insert the seedling in the hole and press the soil firmly around the base of it so that the roots make contact with the soil. Firmly, by the way, means just what it says. The children should test how firmly the seedling is in place by pulling on one of the leaves. The leaf might tear, but the plant should not budge out of the ground. Next, the children should make a slight indentation around the base of the seedling to catch water. Then have them measure the spacing to the next plant, and repeat the process.

Once all of the plants have been tucked in, they deserve a drink of water, perhaps with some fertilizer in it, and then perhaps a light mulch of hay or straw to further protect the plants from the sun and wind. Make sure the children don't forget to label the seedlings or rows with the variety and planting date. Also, indicate on the garden plan the date and weather conditions on the day of transplanting.

The first days of garden life

The first couple of days can make or break the plant. To avoid having to guard the plants day in and day out, I now rely on floating row covers and black plastic (see the sidebar on p. 81) to provide that protection.

Most commonly used by commercial farmers, a floating row cover is a feather-light, spun fiber covering that will prevent cold air from damaging seedlings, will retain warmth, and will keep birds, animals, and insects out. One year I planted tomato and cucumber plants a bit early in what turned out to be an unusually cool spring. I was worried, but the row covers kept these plants toasty and safe. With transplants, I use row covers only for a couple of weeks, until temperatures are stable and the seedlings have become established. I keep these covers on until the plant foliage pushes against them.

Be careful, though, when the temperatures start going up. Keeping the row covers on too long, and therefore increasing the air temperature under the cover, can ruin cool-loving crops like lettuce and spinach. Row covers can also be used with direct-seeded plants to keep munching animals away. It works wonders.

CHAPTER SIX

Tending the Garden

Once the garden has been planted, the waiting begins. But waiting does not mean simply sitting back and watching the vegetables and fruit grow. On the contrary, the plants will need your children's help to mature and thrive. The garden will require regular maintenance, including watering, weeding, controlling pests, and cleaning, as well as a good amount of thinning and pruning. To provide children with season-long harvesting and planting, you can also extend the growing season by having the children complete some simple projects. All this work you and the children do during the season will result in an abundant harvest at the end of the season.

Once the seedlings are in the ground, you should let the children know that the work has really just begun. But the work doesn't need to be tedious. Instead, the children's gardening experience can be designed so that they enjoy what they are doing. Let's take a look at some ways to make these tasks fun and interesting for the children.

Tending the vegetable garden is an enjoyable way for children and adults to spend time outdoors together.

Black plastic and organic mulch, such as hay, can reduce the amount of watering you and the children will need to do.

Watering the Garden

Children love to play with water and hoses, so watering comes as a natural outgrowth of these interests. I love to watch my two boys water the lawn and garden. Usually, swimsuits are *de rigeur*, and large water blasters join the garden hose as a water war typically breaks out. The by-products of my family's water wars—in which my husband plays as big a part as the boys—are a well-soaked lawn, a nicely watered garden, and exhausted children. In my mind, the perfect combination on a lazy summer night.

But there's a lot more to watering than just breaking out the hose and squirting the plants. As an organic gardener—and therefore as a person who values the earth's resources—I believe it's important to conserve water. That means explaining the importance of conservation to the children as well as explaining to them when they need to water and how.

Conservation

Let's first address the issue of planning a garden to avoid the excess use of water. Many people, particularly those of us who depend on well water, have a vested interest (often largely financial and environmental) in using as little water as possible. This topic should be a point of discussion with your children when you first plant the garden, so that they may focus on ways to avoid the excess use of water.

To minimize your use of water, I encourage you to use black plastic (see p. 81) or organic mulch, such as weed-free hay or straw. (If the hay or straw has weeds, the children will simply be planting weeds in the garden when they lay the mulch.) These materials will not only reduce the amount of watering you and the children do but also reduce the amount of weeding (more on weeding later). The mulch will also break down over time, adding organic matter to the soil. When adding mulch, make sure it doesn't come right up to the stems of the vegetable plants, or you and the children will end up with slug and little critter damage.

Another method of conserving water is to use an irrigation system, which will manage the amount of water distributed to the garden. The simplest and most efficient irrigation system for home gardeners is a soaker hose, available at most garden centers and hardware stores. What makes a soaker hose simple is that you just turn the

Parents have to show children how to water. It's important to keep the nozzle on a fine mist to avoid damaging the delicate plants.

water on and off at the spigot—that's it. No aggravation. A soaker hose is more efficient than a watering can or sprayer in that it delivers the water directly to the soil and, in turn, to plant roots.

If you use a soaker hose, turn it so that the holes are facing down toward the ground. This way, no water will be lost to evaporation, and the children won't be tempted to hop through its fine mist, squashing seedlings as they go. Also, be sure to locate the garden near a water spigot.

By using black plastic, organic mulch, and irrigation systems, you will make a significant dent in the amount of watering that will have to be done. But

the plants still need water, so let's talk about the best time for the children to water and how to do it.

When and how to water

Watering a garden seems simple enough to children. They grab a hose, turn on the water as high as it will go, aim at the plants, and clamp down on the nozzle to create the strongest stream possible. But if you don't teach your children the correct method of watering and allow them to "pressure wash" the plants, you'll stand by as the plants bend and break under the intense water pressure and as

Because of special needs, some plants need to be watered individually with a watering can.

quickly. Also, any droplets sitting on the leaves could magnify the sun's rays and burn the leaves. The best time to water is first thing in the morning or in the early evening after the sun has gone down. Translated into child time, this means before school or camp or after dinner.

Your watering method depends on what is being watered. For instance, newly transplanted seedlings need to be watered with a sprayer set on a gentle mist, with a hand-held watering can, or with a soaker hose. If you use black plastic to prevent weeds and conserve water, plants will have to be watered individually so that you can be sure the water gets into a plant's opening in the plastic; otherwise, water will be wasted on top. To water an entire garden, you can use a hose with an adjustable nozzle so that you can control the flow, or you can use a soaker hose.

If you plan on watering with a garden hose and spray nozzle, a rule of thumb to pass on to the children is, when in doubt, mist. When you first take the children outside to water the garden, point out how delicate the plants are. Use a young weed growing nearby to demonstrate how a powerful stream of water can hurt a young plant. Then teach them how to spray the plants with a gentle mist, carefully watching the reaction of the plants. If the plants begin to bend, tell the children to make the mist even more fine.

Explain to the children that water must penetrate deep enough to reach the roots. Many children will end their watering task once the soil looks wet

well-worked soil spatters around the garden. That's why it's important to teach children the right way to water.

In general, how frequently the garden needs water will depend on the climate in which you live and on the plants you grow. Most often, children will want to water the garden when it's really hot, strictly as a means of cooling off and tormenting younger siblings. However, watering during the hottest part of the day—between 10 A.M. and 2 P.M. when the sun is strongest—will cause the garden great pain. The water will be wasted because it will evaporate on top. But the job is not finished. Encourage the children to spray again until the garden is thoroughly watered. But don't overwater—indicated by large puddles on the surface—because too much water can give the plants "wet feet," resulting in root decay and dead plants. Have the children test the soil's wetness by sticking their little fingers into the soil. If they feel any dry soil, the garden needs more water.

Weeding

Weeding is a necessity if you and your children are to have healthy, thriving plants. Now, I am one of the curious types of gardeners who happens to enjoy weeding (really, I do). Children, however, tend not to enjoy this chore. To encourage the children to help out, explain why weeding is important and help them identify weeds in the garden. Once they understand the reasons for weeding and can tell a weed from a good plant, try to find ways to lessen the tedium of this task.

Why weeding is important

To help the children understand why they must weed, explain to them that weeds will compete for space, light, water, and nutrients with the fruits and vegetables in the garden (the good plants). This kind of competition will make the children's plants weak and could deplete their harvest. Weeds also tend to house numerous insects and diseases.

Weeds grow fast, which allows them to take space and light from the good plants. This kind of dominance in the garden will significantly slow the growth of good plants and will likely cause the harvest to be decreased and, at times, nonexistent.

Weeds also rob good plants of water and nutrients. They often have deep or pervasive root systems that can choke or dry out the good plants around them. As an example of a harmful root system, find a dandelion plant in your

If black plastic is used in the garden, water plants individually with a watering can. This way, the water can get to the plant roots through the holes in the plastic.

Children should consult the pictures on the seed packets or in the seed catalogs to help tell the difference between the good plants and the weeds.

garden or lawn and have the children attempt to pull it out. Even a young dandelion will have a root 4 in. or 5 in. long—a mature dandelion can sport a root up to 8 in. long. Help the children extract a dandelion with some garden tools so that they can view the whole main root and gain an appreciation for the thievery of water and nutrients that the dandelion can perpetrate.

Identifying weeds

Once the children know why weeds have to be removed, you must teach them how to identify these harmful plants. Identifying some weeds is quite

easy. Dandelions, grasses, and clovers, for instance, are distinctly different from the plants your children will be nurturing. However, some weeds and plants, in their immature form, look very much alike.

To help the children differentiate weeds from good plants, plant the garden in rows (for more on planting in rows, see Chapter 5). If a garden is planted in rows, you can tell the children that any plant growing in the wrong place is a weed. It will also help the children to have a seed packet or catalog in hand while they weed. The picture on the seed packet or in the catalog will help the children identify the good plant and eliminate the weeds.

If you have older children, introduce them to a gardening guide with good illustrations or pictures of weeds so they can identify these harmful plants.

But weeds may not be the only harmful plant that finds a home in the garden. If you live in a treed area, tree seedlings are bound to sprout, particularly those from maple trees. The whirligigs that float down from the tree and look simply stunning stuck on a child's nose will turn into thousands of little "treelings" just waiting to overrun your garden. Have the children pull out these pesky treelings as soon as they discover them, since the treelings send out a strong root system very quickly.

Also, help the children find and pick out any diseased plants that inhabit the garden. These plants must be pulled out before they infect the healthy crops. But before pulling the plant, be sure the damage has not been done by a living creature (I'll talk about identifying pests later in this chapter).

Making weeding less of a chore

The very best way to make weeding less of a chore is to prevent weeds in the first place. To do this, use black plastic (see p. 81) or a 3-in. or 4-in. layer of mulch to cover the ground (keep the mulch away from the plants or harmful critters could have easy access to the stems). Black plastic and mulch will deprive weeds of light and air, preventing their growth. But even with the black plastic and mulch, some weeds are still bound to grow, so weeding still needs to be done.

To make weeding less "chorelike" for your children, try making the job as enjoyable and as easy as possible. Come up with ways to make it fun. I know families that make weeding a game. For instance, last summer, when I was making a garden with a large group of children, I assigned each child involved with the garden a particular weed. It was his or her job to be sure that weed never appeared in the garden. The children weeded whenever they wanted or needed to but only paid attention to one weed, making their responsibility less daunting. Another fun weeding game to play with children is to make it a contest to see which child can pick the most weeds from the garden.

To make the job easier, encourage the children to weed often and when the air is cool and the soil damp. The more often the children weed, the less time they will spend doing the job. Also, young weeds with small roots will come out easier from the damp soil, while pulling mature weeds is more difficult, even with damp soil, because the roots are longer.

It's also critical that you not use weeding as a punishment. If you do, the children will never again associate gardening with good times. A friend I work with talked once about the punishments his father handed out to him and his brothers when they misbehaved. Depending on the offense, his father sentenced the boys to a certain number of hours of weeding in the family garden. When I heard the story, I cringed down to my toes. To this day, my friend says he can't pass a farmstand without feeling his back ache and his neck burn.

Dealing with Pests

Weeds are not the only harmful influence in a garden. Pests, including insects, worms, slugs, and animals, can wreak havoc among the vegetables and fruits you and your children plant. With that in mind, it's critical that the children be able to identify allies and enemies in the garden and learn how to eliminate the enemies. It's also important that they learn how to prevent animals from feasting on their plantings. Of course, because I have made a commitment to organic gardening, none of my pest-management techniques involves the use of chemicals or pesticides (for more on organic pest management, see the sidebar on the facing page). If you need help in conquering any pests, ask your state's Cooperative Extension Service for advice.

Garden allies

Children are fascinated by insects and animals. Some love insects, worms, snakes, and any other kind of crawly thing, and some are completely repelled by them. No matter which category your children fall into, they will be devastated if a swarm of insects begins

Praying mantises will eat a variety of bad insects in the garden, so encourage the children to leave them alone. (Photo by Derek Fell.)

Ladybugs are allies in the garden. They eat aphids, fleas, and other microscopic insects that can destroy your children's plants. (Photo by Ken Druse.)

ORGANIC PEST MANAGEMENT

In Chapter 4, I discussed my attempt to control an onslaught of cucumber beetles with chemical pesticides. I got rid of the beetles, but the vegetables were tainted by the chemicals, which convinced me to become an organic gardener. That means I use organic and noninvasive methods to deal with pests. By adopting these methods yourself, you'll encourage your children to regard their gardening efforts as a natural part of the earth's order, as well as remind them of the responsibility they bear for the future gardens of the world.

To rid gardens of harmful insects, agricultural scientists have developed integrated pest management (IPM) and organic pest management (OPM). IPM combines a variety of methods to prevent pests. Unfortunately, these methods often include spraying with either chemical or organic pesticides.

OPM, on the other hand, builds off the tenets of organic gardening to avoid the use of chemical or organic pesticides altogether. OPM stresses organic soil building, preventive pest control, and proper plant care as methods of dealing with insects. OPM will help your children understand that alternate methods of dealing with insects—other than poisonous chemicals—do exist.

OPM's organic-gardening practices allow you to create a stable balance in your garden, where insects are regulated naturally. In plain child-speak, if you and your family take good care of your plants and soil, you will have fewer problems with insects, weeds, and disease.

What does this all mean to you and your children? It's simple. I have already talked about using compost and natural means of amending your soil, fertilizing, and enhancing the growth of your plants (see Chapter 4). The better soil you have, the healthier plants you will produce and the less inviting your garden will be to insects. Healthy plants attract far fewer insects and are less susceptible

Organic pest management will help ensure a garden full of produce that's free of harmful insects and safe for your family.

to disease. Teach your children to keep their plants healthy so they will remain healthy. For more information about OPM, contact your state's cooperative extension service or an organic farmer's organization.

munching on a plant that was tenderly raised from a seed.

To avoid that horror, first help the children identify the good guys in the garden. It is important to pass on this very critical information, because if your children go on a pest-elimination campaign, they may capture the allies instead of the enemies. Remind them that there are certain creatures that will help control the pests. The chart below provides a list of some garden allies the children should know and leave alone.

GARDEN ALLIES

Creature	Benefits
Dragonflies	Eat midges, mites, and mosquitoes.
Earthworms	Create passageways that carry air and moisture to plant roots. Their waste contains valuable plant nutrients.
Frogs and toads	Eat cutworms, larvae, maggots, mosquitoes, and slugs.
Ground beetles	Munch on cutworms, maggots, slugs, and snails at night.
Ladybugs	Eat such evil pests as aphids, fleas, and other microscopic bad insects.
Praying mantises	Eat aphids, some caterpillars, and whiteflies.
Spiders	Regularly crave pest larvae and insect eggs.

Enemies of the garden

Once the children understand which creatures are good, it's time to show them which ones are bad and explain how to rid the garden of these unwanted pests. Keep in mind, though, that there are more pests out there than I can go over in this chapter. So encourage your children to research and read about insects and other pests, perhaps creating a glossary of them and the plants they devour. Such a list, complete with pictures, will help the children and you deal with these unwanted pests.

Becoming garden detectives

To help identify when there is a pest problem, the children must become garden detectives. They need to identify certain symptoms and characteristics to pick out the correct pest to eliminate. Only when the children have correctly identified the pest can they institute an appropriate plan to rid the garden of that pest. Here are some suggestions to pass on to your children for conducting a garden investigation.

Examine the entire plant, as well as its garden neighbors, for evidence of pest wrongdoing. What part of the plant is affected? Is it just one plant or the entire row of similar plants? Are nonsimilar plants affected as well? Does the destruction follow a pattern or is it entirely random, such as only the stalks being gnawed or just the tender new growth being chewed?

Tomato hornworms will chomp a good amount of leaves and fruit if you don't catch them in time. (Photo by Ken Druse.)

Colorado potato beetles not only munch on potato leaves but also cause significant damage to tomatoes and eggplants. (Photo by Derek Fell.)

Look at every part of the plant, and don't forget under the leaves! In this hard-to-examine spot, the children may find insects, their eggs, or even disease spores. Give each child a small magnifying glass to really look for the pests and any damage to plants. Last year, my family grew broccoli that, overnight, appeared with dissipated leaves. No matter how hard the children looked, they couldn't find a bit of evidence on the plant. Being the experienced garden mom that I am (and having lost numerous broccoli plants to pests), I handed the children a small magnifying glass. There, under the leaves and attached to the stalks, sat several well-fed cabbage worms that were, much to the children's surprise, the *exact* color of the broccoli plant! The magnifying glass, together with the examination of the leaves' undersides, helped the children find these ravenous, emerald-colored pests.

Eliminating pests

When pests have been found, you and the children first need to capture them, identify them, and then come up with a plan to combat them.

Many pests simply can be handpicked from the plants once they have been discovered. For instance, hornworms are ugly, large, white-striped caterpillars that can frustrate a tomato gardener. Fortunately, hornworms are easy to spot and, quite surprisingly, easy to

A garden detective uses a magnifying glass to search plants for clues of insect damage.

control. Although they look like something you would never want to touch, just handpick and kill them.

Although large creatures can be caught by hand, smaller insects or those that come out at night may require other means of capture. To that end, handy insect catchers can be constructed with a couple of small cans—tuna and cat-food cans work well—and a bit of screening. If you prefer to buy insect catchers, they are available at many educational stores, such as The Nature Company.

Once the pests have been captured, have the children use a good insect book to identify them (these types of books are available at educational stores and libraries) and then write down all pertinent information about the pest in a garden journal. They should include such information as symptoms of infestation, type of pest, and how to eliminate it. This way, when the children encounter the pest in

Symptoms	Possible pests	Solutions
Stippled yellow or pale leaves with:		
Fine webbing underneath	Spider mites	Soap sprays
Silverlike sheen	Thrips	Bright blue or yellow sticky traps
Blotchy patterns and spots or excrement	Lace bugs	Soap sprays
Small holes in leaves with cleanly cut edges	Flea beetles	Floating row covers
Large holes in leaves and veins with:		
Green droppings on leaves	Caterpillars or cabbage worms	Handpick and destroy (wood ash or lime around plant stems prevents egg laying)
Shiny trails	Slugs or snails	Place collars around stems or use small cans with beer to trap them
No further clues	Beetles, worms, or animals	Fencing and floating row covers
Puckered, twisted leaves or growing tips	Aphids	Strong spray of water
Leaves rolled up with webbing inside	Leafrollers	Handpick and destroy
Leaves look like skeletons with only veins remaining	Japanese or Mexican bean beetles	Floating row covers
Leaves with curving white trails	Leafminers	Remove infested leaves
Roots that have been chewed	Rootworms or grubs	Rotate crops
Roots with tunnels and rot in them	Root maggots	Tar-paper squares
Healthy seedling stems cut crisply with:		
Trail of silver mucus on soil	Slugs or snails	Place collars around stems or use small cans with beer to trap them
No trail	Cutworms	Handpick and destroy or place collars around stems

Crow eyes will keep crows, blue jays, seagulls, and other birds away from the garden.

most common methods are with a scarecrow or crow eyes. Scarecrows look like human beings to birds, especially if there are ribbons or arms flapping in the wind. The bird's natural fear of humans will therefore keep them away. Crow eyes are large, balloon-like items that have big eyes painted on them. The eyes make birds think that predators are watching them, thus scaring them away.

If you live near fields or woods, deer can be your undoing. Deer have quite a taste for just about any garden plant and have the ability to wipe out your garden in a night or two. They tend to feed between dusk and dawn, when you are least likely to see them, so devise some preventive measures that will work even if you are asleep. Fencing, cages for certain plants, hanging soap bars, and a mixture of blood meal, garlic, and hot sauce distributed around the garden perimeter can all be effective deer repellents.

Smaller animals, such as chipmunks, squirrels, mice, and rabbits, can be kept out of the garden with blood meal sprinkled around the perimeter or around plants. I have successfully used it to protect bulbs, onions, and potatoes (as an added benefit, blood meal is a terrific source of phosphorus, a necessary plant nutrient).

Fencing will keep some small animals, as well as most midsize animals—such as raccoons, armadillos, woodchucks, and skunks—out of the garden. To help keep smaller animals out, a combination of fencing and row covers may be needed to protect tender seedlings, which seem to be a very tasty

future years, they'll be able to find and eliminate it quickly. (The chart on p. 95 describes the symptoms of and solutions to some of the common pests you and your children might become acquainted with.)

Animal pests

Insects are certainly not the only pests children need to be aware of. Both birds and four-legged beasts can also do a lot of damage in a garden quickly.

There are many ways to keep blue jays, crows, and seagulls from landing in and eating your garden. Two of the treat for little creatures. By the time the row covers are removed, the plants will not be as appealing to the animals, and they will find other sources of food.

If you have a significant problem with animal pests, consider humane traps that do not harm the animal or consult your local animal-control officer for assistance. If you choose to capture and release the animals, check local laws regarding their release. Some towns prohibit you from releasing an animal in another area. For safety reasons, trapping animals is not recommended for children.

Pest prevention

The simplest method of dealing with pests is to keep them away from the plants in the first place. The best way to keep pests out of the garden is to keep it clean. But pest prevention may also require the use of physical barriers, such as stem collars, some careful detective work at the nursery, and companion planting.

Keep it clean

Even if your children can't keep their rooms clean, they should understand that cleanliness will make a large difference in the health of their plants. So encourage the children to keep the garden clean: have them eliminate any diseased plants immediately, weed often, and keep tools and hands clean.

Pulling weeds as soon as they sprout, or using black plastic or mulch to prevent weeds, will help the children thwart the arrival of insect pests that enjoy garden plants as a side dish while they primarily munch on the weeds.

A clean garden helps prevent pests and allows children to eat their harvest straight from the plant.

Good garden sanitation spreads to the children's garden tools, as well as to their hands. Encourage the children to clean their garden tools regularly, using hot, soapy water at least a couple of times during the season and especially always after working with diseased plants. If the children use garden gloves, be sure they toss the gloves into the washing machine after handling pests or diseased plants. If the children work without gloves, remind them to wash their hands midway through their

COMPANION PLANTS

Companion plant	Pests repelled or attracted	Plant with
Dill	Tomato hornworms	Tomatoes
Garlic	Japanese beetles, tomato hornworms	Corn, lettuce, peas, tomatoes
Horseradish	Colorado potato beetle	Potatoes
Marigolds	Nematodes, tomato hornworms, whiteflies	Tomatoes
Mints	Flea beetles, tomato hornworms, cabbage worms and beetles	Tomatoes, cabbage, radishes
Nasturtium	Aphids, squashbugs, whiteflies	Apple trees, parsley, squash
Sweet basil*	Aphids, mites, mosquitoes	Sweet peppers and tomatoes
Thyme	Cabbage maggots, flea beetles, imported cabbage worms, white cabbage butterflies	Broccoli, brussels sprouts, cabbage

Can also work as an organic fungicide when spread around plants.

garden work if they have been picking pests off plants or handling diseased leaves or fruit.

Physical barriers

Some of the more common barriers to pests are floating row covers, fencing, and traps, which I've already discussed. These methods work for many pests but might not be enough to prevent others from reaching the plant stalks. To add another barrier to pests at the plants, you and the children can plant young seedlings within collars made from aluminum cans, cardboard, or plastic.

For example, cutworms can be a tomato gardener's nightmare because they like to munch on the stalk of the plant, which will kill it quickly. To prevent the cutworms from reaching the stalk, cut out both ends of a clean soup can and place the seedling's root ball through the can. Then bury about half of the can in the soil. The can will serve as a protective collar for the lower stalk of the plant. Collars from cardboard or plastic also work, but the children can recycle the cans after the growing season or clean them and save them for next year.

Marigolds are perfect companion plants for tomatoes, helping to protect the precious fruit from tomato hornworms, nematodes, and whiteflies.

Garden detectives to the rescue

Oftentimes, pests are brought into the garden via purchased seedlings. So it's important that you and the children examine the seedlings very carefully. In fact, the visit to the farmer's market or nursery is a good time for the children to hone their garden-detective skills. Bring along a few magnifying glasses and have the children conduct an investigation. Be sure they do not buy plants infected with disease or infested with pests (for more on buying seedlings, see pp. 76-77).

Companion planting

Companion planting is a natural method of pest control. The technique has its basis mostly in folklore rather than in science, but if it works, both you and the garden benefit.

Companion planting primarily relies on scent—something smelly is planted near a vegetable plant and the insects will either be repelled by or attracted to the smelly plant. Children, who seem to have a fine appreciation for smelly stuff, will love this notion. Many companion plants are lovely flowers, which the children can integrate artistically into the garden.

Pruning the suckers from a tomato stem allows the plant to send more nutrients to the fruit-producing branches, thus increasing the harvest.

The chart on p. 98 lists some common companion plants, along with the insects they repel or attract. Keep in mind that what works in one area may not work in another, so ask fellow gardeners around your town and state—particularly master gardeners or organic farmers at the market—about what companion plants work well in your area.

Thinning and Pruning Plants for a Better Harvest

I have always had the hardest time convincing children that the best way to grow better plants was to grow fewer of them. Many children believe that more is better. For instance, if one radish seed in an inch is good, then 20 in an inch must be better. However, this is not true when it comes to gardening. That's why it's important to make thinning and pruning a regular part of garden maintenance. Both of these jobs will help the garden produce healthy, strong plants, which in turn will make for a better harvest.

Thinning

As I mentioned in Chapter 5, thinning is the process of pulling out weak plants from a row to make room for the stronger ones. Regardless of whether you and the children transplanted seedlings to the garden or direct seeded, plants may grow larger than you expected and could crowd other plants around it. This could cause plants to compete for light, water, and nutrients, which will hurt all the plants involved in the struggle. For such root crops as carrots, thinning means the difference between a fully grown carrot and a stunted, deformed one that lacked sufficient space to grow.

You and the children first started thinning when you separated the young seedlings indoors (see p. 71). When plants are in the garden, encourage the children to thin when plants are near mid-maturity. At this point, the plants are strong enough to pull out cleanly but small enough that this action will not greatly disturb the other plants. Teach the children to look for the smallest, weakest plants that are near strong, healthy ones. Then show them how to grasp the small plants by the stem, close to the ground, and gently but firmly pull the plant out.

Don't let plants removed during the thinning process go to waste. Have the children throw them into the compost pile for recycling or, perhaps, the plants can be brought directly to the dinner table. For instance, if you are thinning lettuce, spinach, onions, or chard, the baby leaves from these plants are a delicacy that many of us would pay dearly for during the winter.

Pruning

Pruning is another method for the children to strengthen their plants. Pruning prevents the plant from growing too large and from directing energy and nutrients to leaves or branches instead of to the fruit or vegetable. By snipping off unnecessary branches, you and your children will help the plant redirect its efforts to the important work at hand: providing an abundant harvest.

Let's use tomatoes as a prime example. Tomatoes shoot out suckers (small branches that produce no blossoms) all over the place, which can rob the plant of much-needed nutrients and strength. Suckers will appear in great abundance toward the bottom part of the plant, with some near the top. Children can use their small fingers to snap off the suckers that grow between the main stem and the primary leaf branches. But be sure they leave a few of the suckers found on the top of the plant to shield the fruit from sunscald, a condition that produces light-gray patches on the tomatoes and can cause the fruit to become subject to disease. By keeping a watchful eye on their tomato plants and carefully pruning suckers when they appear, the children can speed up their tomato harvest by up to two weeks.

Extending the Growing Season

The children are watering, weeding, fighting pests, thinning and pruning, all the while waiting for the harvest. More than likely, by midseason you will be hit with cries of, "Isn't there anything else to do?" (interpreted most often as, "Isn't there anything more to plant?"). Well, there probably is. Each

The harvest is the best part of gardening. Children love to wash the veggies they just plucked from the garden.

because you'll end up with tough or bitter produce.

All the necessary planting information for cool- and warm-weather crops can be found in seed catalogs or on seed packets. This information should also be included in the plant data sheets the children created during the planning stage of the garden (see Chapter 1).

Short- and long-season crops

Another interplanting technique is growing long- and short-season crops together in the same row or bed. Growing successive crops in this manner allows the children to space the plants closer together than usual, since short-season crops are harvested and removed by the time the longer-season

crops need the growing space. The children can replant short-season crops for a much later harvest or introduce a completely different plant into the very same garden space. For instance, onions planted in the early spring can be harvested by mid-spring, leaving room for the children to plant corn.

When interplanting, match shallow-rooting plants with deep-rooting plants to allow both types to get the most out of the soil. The shallow roots draw moisture and nutrients from the top soil zones, while the deep roots draw from the lower zones. Try pairing onions with tomatoes, leeks with carrots, and Swiss chard or kale with parsnips.

Also, try to use the natural properties of the plants to achieve a better harvest. For instance, growing maturing corn plants near low-growing, cool-weather plants like lettuce, parsley, radishes, and spinach, will keep these plants cool and conserve moisture in the soil.

Use the sample successive planting schedule on p. 103 to help you and your children through your first season or two of interplanting. The schedule is based on seasonal temperature points. You and your children can determine the time in your region that corresponds to the season described.

Harvesting

All of the patience, research, and careful tending the children do to raise healthy plants pays off at harvest time. In the weeks leading up to harvest, children will be giddy with anticipation as they watch fruit and vegetables form. After

With a quick rinse, this baby lettuce and mesclun will become a fresh dinner salad.

giving some simple directions about when and how to pick, sit back to watch your children delight in the fruits of their labor.

Harvesting for children may be an exercise in restraint or one of diligence. In general, it's best to pick fruit and vegetables as soon as they are ripe. Underripened fruit and vegetables have not achieved their full taste potential, resulting in a bland or bitter taste. Overripened fruit and vegetables tend to become tough or rotten and can rob newly formed fruit and vegetables of valuable water and nutrients. Overripened produce can also attract pest insects.

How the children harvest will depend on the type of plant. Root crops, such as carrots, will have to be completely removed from the ground (one carrot at a time). Other plants, such as tomatoes and cucumbers, can be harvested by gently picking only the ripened fruit or vegetable from a vine or stem. Broccoli plants, on the other hand, will continue to produce if you cut the edible stalks as they appear and keep tending the plant.

Be sure to spend a lot of time with your children during the first harvest. They'll need your gardening expertise to help them along. Good instructions about harvesting can also be found on the seed packets or in the seed catalogs from which you ordered. If you purchased your seedlings from a nursery or farmer's market, make sure to ask when harvesting is appropriate for each plant and how to do it. A reasonable project for the children during the growing season and between watering and weeding, is to conduct some harvesting research for all of their plants and record this information on the plant data sheets they prepared before the season (see Chapter 1).

Putting the Garden to Bed

The last project the children will have in the garden itself will be cleaning it up for the winter and preparing the soil for next year's garden.

To preserve the health of the garden for next year, it is important that they clean the garden well, disposing of rotted fruit, plants gone by, and weeds. (Remember that any diseased or pest-infested plants should not be placed in the compost pile.). Keeping the garden clean also clears the garden of cozy hideaways for unwanted pests.

Many gardening professionals believe that late fall is the most important time on the gardening calendar, because it's time the soil should be prepared for the next season's plantings. If we instill this belief in our children, they will learn that completing the last task of one season is also completing the first of the next season. "Cool!" said my oldest son. "We get double credit for something five months away!"

Amend the soil

The late fall is a good time to add organic matter to the soil. The organic matter will decompose slowly into the soil all winter long. Have the children test the pH level of the soil and determine what soil additions are necessary (for more on soil testing, see Chapter 4). After a full harvest, the pH usually drops to near 5.5, so you may need to raise it up into the high sixes again (perhaps by adding ground limestone). Also, encourage the children to add fresh cow manure, if you can get it, together with any usable compost left over from the summer's supply. Gardens that have heavy soil can use a layer of peat moss to help build up the organic matter.

After the organic amendments have been added, rent a small rototiller and work with the children to mix these amendments well into the soil. Small tillers are usually not too unwieldy and can be handled—with supervision—by most children in their teens.

Plant a winter cover crop

Once the amendments have been worked into the soil, suggest to the children that they plant a winter cover crop (or a crop that will be harvested in the early spring, such as garlic—see the sidebar on the facing page). A winter cover crop helps maintain the soil quality and prevent erosion during wet winter weather.

Winter rye grass is a wonderful cover crop. It will sprout quickly and remain green for most of the winter, giving the garden a living color instead of the dead brown associated with winter. In the spring, as soon as the soil dries out, the children can use a small tiller to turn under the rye grass, providing an excellent organic addition to the spring soil.

THE FALL AND WINTER VEGETABLE GARDEN

After you and your children have amended the garden's soil at the end of the season, you might consider planting a few vegetables that will grow during the fall and winter, such as garlic and parsnips. These plants will sprout in the early spring, signaling to the children that the time to garden has arrived.

I have found that fall-planted garlic is bigger and more flavorful than that planted in spring. Many seed and bulb houses will ship your garlic very late in the summer, so the bulbs will not rot during the summer heat. The garlic my children plant in the fall inevitably pushes through the garden in March, just as the spring crocuses begin to grow and bloom.

Winter is the time for spring-planted parsnips to sweeten. The longer a parsnip stays in the cold ground, the sweeter it will be. To protect parsnips from very cold weather, add a layer of mulch before a frost. As soon as the soil thaws in early spring, you can dig up the parsnips and enjoy their sweet taste.

While this year's garden is blooming, have the children look for crops that can be harvested in the spring. It's a wonderful way for the children to continue researching

Plant parsnips in the spring and harvest them the following March as soon as the soil thaws.

plant choices during the summer. A few good sources for this type of information are seed catalogs and packets, nurseries, farmers, and master gardeners.

Making Gardening Fun for Children

As I've emphasized throughout the first section of this book, it's important to maintain your children's interest in the garden by making the activities enjoyable. And that's what this section is all about.

Here I'll give you some ideas on how to stretch the harvest into other areas of your life and have a good time doing it. I'll show you how to create theme gardens with your children. I'll also illustrate several garden-related activities that can make gardening a means to a holiday or birthday gift for a friend, teacher, or family member.

Don't be limited by what I offer you here. Think about your own children, focusing on what they like to eat and what they like to make, and help them push their creative levels. Go wild with their ideas!

CHAPTER SEVEN

Theme Gardens

Most children love to eat pizza and will enjoy growing the ingredients to make their own special pies.

Adopting a theme for a garden is a terrific way to ease children into gardening. A theme garden provides a maximum amount of fun for the whole family while helping children choose plants by limiting the endless choices available to them.

In this chapter, I have illustrated seven different theme gardens: a pizza garden, pasta garden, snack garden, heritage garden, pet garden, a fall holiday garden, and a garden for winged visitors. Accompanying the discussion of each garden is a plant list and, where appropriate, recipes that can be made from that garden.

Don't feel constrained by the seven gardens discussed here, though. Talk with your children about their interests and hobbies, as well as your family heritage, and design your own theme garden. The research required for each theme garden will allow the children (and, perhaps, you) to discover plants, folklore, and foods they never knew existed.

Whether you choose to create one of these theme gardens or make your own, be sure the children keep a journal about the garden. Have them list the plants that went into it as well as the reasons behind choosing that particular theme. During the season, the children can keep notes in the journal about the garden, indicating any problems and their solutions along with other planting or harvesting information. This kind of journal makes wonderful reading to a classroom or a kitchen full of friends on a cold winter afternoon.

The Pizza Garden

No other food than pizza could possibly appear first in a book about gardening with children. In my house, pizza is a dinner mainstay, and homemade pizza is a family project with considerable discussion about not only which vegetables will go on the pizza but also who will roll out the dough, how many cheeses will be used, and whether there is enough root beer in the house to wash down all the pizza we will surely eat. As far as foods go, pizza is not an unhealthy favorite, either. If you make the pizza yourself, you can control the amount of fat and provide your children with whole grains, fresh vegetables, protein, and a good deal of taste.

I have found pizza to be a great way to expand my children's taste buds. For instance, feta cheese or goat cheese takes on a whole new flavor when sprinkled on top of a pizza brimming with garden-grown produce. Any vegetable tastes better when it's a topping on a homemade pizza pie. My family's pizza toppings have included spinach, red peppers, arugula, plenty of fresh basil, and zucchini. If a vegetable

	PLANTS FOR A PIZZA GARDEN	
Plant	**Use**	**Comments**
Plum tomatoes ('La Rossa')	Sauce and topping	Will not vine and may not need to be staked. Are small with thick, dry flesh.
Parsley (flat leaf)	Chopped in sauce to add flavor and color	Will winter over in cold climates if well mulched or if planted in a warm, protected spot.
Oregano (Greek only!)	Flavoring in sauce	Can take over a garden in just one growing season. Needs to be clipped frequently.
Garlic (softneck or stiffneck)	Sauce and topping	Can be planted in fall or spring. Fall planting ensures larger, more flavorful heads.
Peppers ('Bull's Horn' or 'Lipstick')	Topping	Let mature until red for best flavor.
Onions (red storage or mini white or red)	Sauce and topping	Minis appear early in the garden.
Sweet basil	Chopped in sauce	Purchase seedlings and grow in hot sun. Harvest often.

I hosted a pizza party at the peak of the summer harvest. The party featured fresh-picked toppings and sauce made from my children's tomatoes.

grows in the garden, it has appeared on a pizza in my house, and—better yet—the children have actually eaten it.

A pizza garden is a terrific way for your children to get involved in gardening. The harvest from a pizza garden will provide the whole family with wonderful heart- and stomach-warming experiences. Let's focus on two distinct goals from a pizza garden: the ingredients for the sauce and the vegetable toppings. (See the chart on p. 111 for a list of plants suitable for a pizza garden. A couple of recipes are on the facing page.)

Tomato sauce from the garden

Homemade tomato sauce brings pizza to a new level—one your children will relish. Tomato sauce for pizza is typically a basic Italian red sauce with an abundance of oregano, basil, parsley, and, usually, garlic.

Sauces tend to be chunky or smooth. If you and your children prefer chunky sauce, during the growing season you can pick fresh produce from the garden and create a chunky sauce that is fresh tasting and delicious.

PIZZA-GARDEN RECIPES

Almost-Traditional Pizza

1 envelope dry yeast
about 1 cup warm water
4 cups flour: 3 cups unbleached white,
    1 cup whole wheat
2 tablespoons extra-virgin olive oil
2 tablespoons cornmeal
1 cup tomato sauce
1½ cups grated mozzarella cheese
preferred vegetable toppings

Dissolve the yeast in ½ cup warm water. Mix the flours in a large bowl. Make a well in the center of the flour and add dissolved yeast. Add enough of the remaining warm water to make a soft dough.

Knead the dough until soft and elastic. Cover with a towel and let rise in a warm place until doubled in volume. When doubled, punch down the dough and press and stretch (don't roll) it out into a circle about ½ in. thick on a floured board. Oil a pizza stone or heavy cookie sheet, sprinkle with cornmeal, and place the dough onto it.

Cover with sauce and toppings and bake at 450°F until crust is light brown and cheese is bubbling.

Fresh Tomato Sauce

3 tablespoons extra-virgin olive oil
3 large cloves garlic, squeezed in
    a press
4 cups seeded and chopped plum
    tomatoes
3 tablespoons chopped fresh oregano
salt, to taste
black pepper, to taste
2 tablespoons chopped fresh basil

Heat the olive oil in a heavy skillet over low heat. Add the garlic and sauté gently 1–2 minutes. Do not brown the garlic.

Add the tomatoes, oregano, salt, and pepper and cook 5 minutes, stirring occasionally. Stir in the chopped basil and cook 1–2 minutes longer, stirring constantly. Serve immediately with pasta or cool it for use later on pizza.

If you want to duplicate smooth sauce that you might find in a jar, you can still use fresh-picked produce, but you'll have to simmer the sauce quite a while to get a smooth and thick consistency. This effort will let the children experience how much cooking is really involved in creating such a sauce and that real vegetables do actually make it into jars found in the grocery store.

Whether you choose chunky or smooth sauce, you will need to plant a good sauce tomato, which is known as

Children can come up with a number of interesting pizza toppings, including cherry tomatoes, grated carrots, and chard.

a plum or paste tomato. You should also have oregano in your garden, as well as garlic, basil, and onions.

Pizza toppings for the picking

Many of the ingredients for sauce, such as tomatoes, onions, and garlic, may also be used as toppings. There are a host of other vegetables that sit very well indeed on top of the sauce. Any good pizza garden will include peppers—both sweet green and red—spinach, scallions, zucchini, and summer squash. Just about anything you and your children can grow in the garden can go on a pizza (well, maybe not the potatoes). Talk with your children to decide what they must have and what they would like to try on a pizza, then plant away.

To make planting a pizza garden more fun, plant a circular garden that resembles a pizza pie, with each "slice" growing a particular vegetable or herb (see the drawing on the facing page). To make the garden, begin by laying out

A Pizza-Shaped Garden

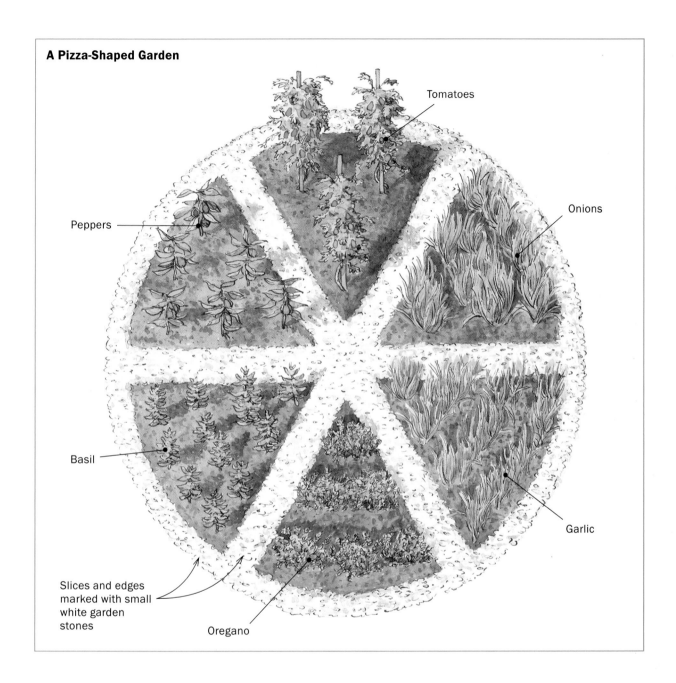

Tomatoes

Onions

Peppers

Basil

Garlic

Slices and edges
marked with small
white garden
stones

Oregano

the circular design. Attach a length of string to a 3-ft. stake. Drive the stake in the center of the garden area. Stretch the string out the desired distance and tie another stake to it. Pull the string taut and drag the stake in the soil, marking the perimeter. Then divide the circle into slices, mark them with small white garden stones, and plant. By midseason, you and the children will have a garden beautiful to both the eye and the mouth.

My basil pesto usually gets a thumbs-up from the children.

Pasta Garden

In my house, pasta is the number-two favorite food (after pizza). Because both my husband and I work, we rely on pasta with various sauces for a meal at least once or twice a week. The three favorites in my house are tomato (see the recipe on p. 113), basil pesto, and uncooked tomato sauce. You could also create a meal simply by topping pasta with an assortment of fresh-picked vegetables.

We make basil pesto during the growing season (see the recipe on p. 118) and store it in the refrigerator, covered with olive oil. To use it in pasta meals, we drain off the olive oil (into a jar for use on salads or cooking), scoop out the pesto, add fresh-grated parmesan or Romano cheese, and mix it all into hot pasta. The smell alone of pesto being made makes the children think "summer."

When the summer temperatures are at their highest, there's nothing more refreshing than a pasta meal covered with uncooked tomato sauce (see the recipe on p. 118). This meal is easy to make and will save you the agony of standing over a simmering pot of sauce.

During the gardening season, the toppings for pasta seem to expand dramatically. There is nothing like walking through the garden with your children, looking for what's ripe and what combinations might taste good with some fettuccini, a little grated cheese—well, you get the picture. Last summer my family started calling these garden trips our pasta walks.

There really isn't a vegetable out there that can't be served over pasta. Try peppers, onions, chopped tomatoes (with or without sausage), spinach, arugula, snap peas sautéed in olive oil, zucchini, summer squash, green beans, eggplant, and small carrots to make spring prima vera (see the recipe on p. 118). The possibilities are endless.

Herbs are also welcome additions to a pasta meal. I always had to remind my sons to include the herbs in our pasta walk. They were already lovers of basil but soon discovered that thyme, rosemary, and sage were wonderful complements to the vegetables and sauces we prepared. (See the chart on the facing page for a list of plants suitable for a pasta garden.)

PLANTS FOR A PASTA GARDEN

Plant	Use	Comments
Plum tomatoes ('La Rossa')	For pasta sauces	Will not vine and may not need to be staked.
Garlic (softneck or stiffneck)	For pasta sauces and topping	Can be planted in fall or spring.
Sugar snap peas	Sautéed with spring greens for pasta prima vera	Plant several rows in succession over two or three weeks for steady supply.
Zucchini (striped)	For pasta sauces	Usually the champion producer of garden, so plant just a few for a handsome crop.
Summer squash (yellow)	For pasta sauces	Pick when small and tender, as the larger they get, the tougher they become.
Greens (arugula, broccoli, chard, kohlrabe, sorrel, spinach)	For pasta sauces	These grow quickly and can be picked early.
Eggplant (Elondo)	For pasta sauces	Warm-weather plant that demands full sun. Pick fruit when firm to the touch—the smaller, the better.

Herbs

Plant	Use	Comments
Basil (large leaf or sweet)	As foundation for pesto or chopped with other vegetables, or as seasoning in pasta sauces	Purchase seedlings and grow in hot sun. Harvest often.
Rosemary	As seasoning in pasta sauces	Purchase as seedlings and bring indoors if ground freezes during winter.
Sage	As seasoning in pasta sauces	This perennial is perfect for drying. Hang it in your kitchen for winter use.
Tarragon	As seasoning in pasta sauces	Plant seedlings in well-draining, sunny spot.
Thyme	As seasoning in pasta sauces	Hardy for most climates and is also a pretty garden plant. In medieval France, thyme was planted in children's gardens as a home for fairies.

PASTA · GARDEN RECIPES

Basil Pesto

2 cups fresh basil leaves, washed and dried

4 cloves garlic, peeled

½ cup pine nuts, lightly toasted

1¼ cups fresh-grated parmesan or Romano cheese

½–1 cup extra-virgin olive oil

cracked black pepper, to taste

Finely chop the basil leaves, garlic cloves, and pine nuts in a food processor. With the machine running, pour ½ cup olive oil in a steady, thin stream through the top of the processor. Add oil until the mixture is smooth and batterlike, then stop the machine.

To use immediately, add cheese, season with cracked black pepper to taste, and process to combine. To store, omit cheese and refrigerate (covered with olive oil to keep it fresh). Add cheese before serving. Toss pesto with hot pasta, using ½ cup pesto (or to taste) for 1 pound pasta.

Uncooked Tomato Sauce

10 plum tomatoes or 5 large eating tomatoes, seeded and chopped

2 large cloves garlic

2 tablespoons finely chopped, fresh basil

¼ cup extra-virgin olive oil

salt, to taste

black pepper, to taste

fresh-grated Romano cheese

Place the tomatoes in a deep bowl. Press the garlic cloves directly into the bowl with the tomatoes. Add the basil and olive oil, cracked black pepper to taste, and a pinch of salt. Stir, cover, and let sit 15–20 minutes.

Toss mixture with hot pasta. Cover generously with grated cheese and serve.

Spring Prima Vera

¼ cup extra-virgin olive oil

2 tablespoons butter

2 cups sugar snap peas, cleaned

5–10 Baby carrots, cleaned and sliced

½ cup arugula leaves, washed and trimmed

½ cup spinach leaves, washed and trimmed

4–5 scallions, including greens

1 tablespoon balsamic vinegar (or to taste)

fresh-grated Romano or parmesan cheese

Heat oil and butter over low heat. Add peas and carrots and sauté 2 minutes. Add greens and continue sautéing until greens have wilted. Once greens have wilted, add balsamic vinegar, stir, and simmer 1 minute. Serve over hot pasta with grated cheese to taste.

Snack Garden

My generation was raised to believe that snack foods had to be sweet, prewrapped, and preportioned. But one of my many goals in involving my children in gardening was to introduce some healthy snack alternatives to them.

By planting a snack garden, parents can directly address the issue of healthy eating by asking for our children's direction. The development of a snack garden screams out for a family discussion. Ask everybody to make a list of their favorite snack foods that could come from a garden. Do your best to focus the list on finger foods, since this theme garden will really work if your children can simply go to the garden, pick what they want to eat, wash it, and munch away—no knives or cutting boards involved.

Your family list may include carrots, cucumbers, cherry tomatoes, celery, popcorn, sugar snap peas, and even green beans, all of which are easy to grow and fun to eat right from the garden. After coming up with a list of plants that can be picked and eaten or used as an ingredient in snacks, start planning the garden with your children. By midseason your children will be harvesting and munching healthy, delicious snacks at will. (See the chart below for a list of plants suitable for a snack garden. Some recipes are on p. 120.)

Children love to snack on carrots picked fresh from the garden.

PLANTS FOR A SNACK GARDEN

Plant	Use	Comments
Cherry tomatoes (currants, miniature yellow pear)	Eat straight from the vine or stuffed	Harvest quickly when ripe. Currants are small, and miniature yellow pears are very sweet.
Carrots (Early Chantenay or Baby)	Eat fresh from the garden or with dip	Become tastier as they grow. Harvest as soon as plants are recognizable as carrots.
Cucumbers (pickling)	Eat fresh from the vine	Pick early, when fruit is sweet.
Sugar snap peas	Eat fresh from the vine	Easy to grow and mature in about 55 days from seed planting date. Plant in succession to ensure steady supply.
Popcorn (M212 or Strawberry)	For popping	Homegrown popcorn is sweet, nutty, and delicious—even plain.
Green beans (Haricot Verte)	Eat fresh from the vine or with dip	These are tiny, sweet, and crunchy.

SNACK·GARDEN RECIPES

Stuffed Cherry Tomatoes

1 cup whipped cream cheese

1 small clove garlic, squeezed through a garlic press

1 tablespoon chopped parsley

1 tablespoon finely chopped walnuts (optional)

pinch of salt

2 dozen large cherry tomatoes

To make the stuffing, mix the whipped cream cheese with the pressed garlic clove, the chopped parsley, and the walnuts. Add a pinch of salt.

Slice the tops off the cherry tomatoes and scoop or squeeze out seeds. Add stuffing mixture. Chill or serve immediately.

Ants on a Log

celery stalks, cleaned and cut into 4-inch pieces

peanut butter

raisins or currants

Fill the celery stalks with peanut butter. Place raisins or currants, spaced evenly apart, on top of the peanut butter. Serve immediately, screeching about the ants that have plunked themselves down on the celery. (To make Ants on a Snowy Log, substitute cream cheese, goat cheese, or ricotta cheese for the peanut butter.)

Heritage Garden

The simple act of growing a vegetable spans oceans, cultures, and political beliefs. Whether as a means of decoration, like the formal Japanese tea gardens, as a country's signature, such as the great manor gardens of the British Isles, or in the form of a subsistence garden, every country has gardens, plants, and foods that tie together its heritage and culture. The inquisitive minds of children are ripe for exploring the cultural connections of gardening and food.

Inevitably, children become fascinated with their family's past—the great grandparents they may have never met, the countries from which the family originated, the strange but delicious foods that appear only on special holidays. To help your family research its history, plan a heritage garden. The heritage garden, and the research and planning that families can conduct together before planting, harvesting, and cooking, will bring your family heritage alive for your children. By integrating my family's Albanian heritage into foods and family

Your family will never tire of fresh-made salsa, a staple from a Mexican heritage garden.

traditions, I have helped establish Albania (my grandmother's homeland) as a permanent part of my family's personality.

But you don't have to have a unique or exotic family background to plant a heritage garden. Feel free to adopt another culture as your own. Sit down as a family and discuss everyone's interests. Is Spanish being taught in school with lessons of Mexican history? Is Italian food your family's favorite? Do you know little about Asian culture but quite a bit about your local Thai restaurant? Decide on a country or a type of food that you would like to learn more about or simply taste more of in your own home, then plan away.

Should you decide to research a country outside of your own ethnic background, I encourage you and your family to take advantage of community resources to accomplish your research. Look in your local paper for ethnic festivals or fairs. In my community there is a festival to celebrate the growing immigrant population, where Cambodia, Poland, Korea, and Afghanistan, among many other countries, are well represented in song, dance, and food. With a bit of thought and a quick read of a community newspaper, you and your family can unearth myriad resources for beginning a heritage garden.

Another source of valuable information is an ethnic restaurant. You will be surprised at your children's willingness to try something in a restaurant that they never would even consider at home. Make a meal of several appetizers, trying different

PLANTS FOR A MEXICAN HERITAGE GARDEN

Plant	Use	Comments
Tomatillo (Toma Verde)	Chopped in salsa	Can grow to 5 ft. or 6 ft. tall and produces lots of fruit. Husks that cloak the tender yellow fruit will fascinate children.
Beans (black and pinto)	Add to chili con carne and enchiladas	Growing, drying, and threshing beans is a unique experience for children.
Hot peppers (serrano, otega, poblano, jalapeño)	Use in salsa, burritos, chili con carne, pickling, or stuffing	Plants need warmth and sun. The more red or ripe they get, the hotter the peppers will be.
Corn (field and sweet)	Dry and ground for flour or corn meal	Both field and sweet corn are staples of the Mexican diet.
Herbs		
Epazonte	Use fresh in salads, salsa, or casseroles	Seeds can be found in various seed catalogs.
Cilantro (also known as coriander leaf)	Use fresh in salads, salsa, or casseroles	Seedlings are available at farmer's markets or nurseries.

textures, temperatures, and spices. If your family enjoyed the food, begin researching that country the very next day with a trip to the library or by viewing a video. Consider doing some on-line research with your children or use computer-based encyclopedias.

Researching a Mexican heritage garden

My family chose to make a Mexican heritage garden simply because we all love Mexican food. But Mexico provides us with more than just food. It has a beautiful language, a rich cultural history, and colorful folklore.

To begin the research needed to start a Mexican heritage garden, my family visited a local Mexican restaurant and spoke with the owner, who was from Mexico City. He and his wife were wonderful with the whole family, suggesting foods to try while regaling us with Mexican folklore and songs.

We spoke with a priest who had recently completed a teaching assignment in Mexico. He told colorful stories of the lives of Mexican children and helped us understand quite a bit about Mexican gardens.

We also researched Mexico at our local library, which is full of books about Mexican legends and fables. We were even fortunate in that one of the librarians spent time in Mexico studying Aztec history.

MEXICAN HERITAGE GARDEN RECIPES

Fresh Salsa (Salsa Cruda)

**6–8 plum tomatoes, seeded and
  chopped**
4 tomatillos, chopped fine
1 clove garlic, chopped
1 small onion, chopped
1 small jalapeño pepper, chopped
¼ cup cilantro, chopped
pinch of salt

Mix tomatoes, tomatillos, garlic, onions, and jalapeño in a 1-quart bowl. Pour in the cilantro, a pinch of salt, and stir. Let sit 15 minutes to blend flavors. Serve with tortilla chips and plenty of iced limeade.

Flour Tortillas (Tortilla de Harina)

2 cups unbleached white flour
½ teaspoon baking soda
2 teaspoons salt
**6 tablespoons solid vegetable
  shortening**
6 tablespoons warm water

Sift flour, baking soda, and salt together in a bowl. Cut the shortening into the flour as if for pastry. Add water and make a dough. Knead 5 minutes, adding flour if too wet. Divide into 12 balls and roll into very thin circles on a floured surface. Cook both sides lightly on a hot griddle until lightly brown.

Soft Tacos

2 small chili peppers, chopped
2 large tomatoes, seeded and chopped
1 large onion, chopped
1 large clove garlic
2 tablespoons olive oil
4–6 tortillas, warm (see recipe above)
2 cups black beans, cooked
¼ cup fresh cilantro, chopped
2 cups grated jack cheese

Sauté peppers, tomatoes, onion, and garlic in olive oil until soft. Fill warm tortillas with sautéed mixture and cooked black beans, and garnish with cilantro. Add grated cheese, wrap, heat in a 350°F oven for 10 minutes, and serve with salsa cruda.

**A pet garden is fun for the whole family (especially for the animals!).
Catnip, for instance, is easy to grow and will provide your children's
feline friend with hours of pleasure.**

	PLANTS FOR A PET GARDEN	
Plant	**Animal**	**Comments**
Greens (beet greens, lettuce, spinach)	Rabbits, guinea pigs, some birds	Greens tend to need cool weather and regular watering.
Carrots	Rabbits, horses, donkeys	Need loose soil and a lot of moisture.
Catnip	Cats	Needs lots of sun but cool weather. Grows 18 in. to 36 in. high. Has wacky affect on cats and makes soothing herbal tea for people.
Sunflowers	Birds	Need warmth, sun, and room to grow. The larger plants make better seeds.

We found that the more we let people know what we were doing, the more resources we discovered to aid us in our research. We learned about unique "foodlore," as we called it, finding out that chocolate is the food of kings in Mexico. We decorated our garden with hummingbird feeders after discovering that hummingbirds are sacred in Mexico. A year after growing the Mexican heritage garden, we still eat burritos and enchiladas often, grow our own chiles and cilantro, and make fresh salsa any chance we get. (See the chart on p. 122 for a list of plants suitable for a Mexican heritage garden. Some recipes are on p. 123.)

Pet Garden

A fun garden theme for your children is a pet garden, particularly when the pets include rabbits or guinea pigs, which love fresh greens from the garden, cats, which will crave catnip, or birds, which enjoy sunflower seeds. Your children will delight in picking the crop and presenting the treat to their pet.

The pet garden is also terrific source of gifts for family and friends. The catnip can be dried and stuffed into cat toys. Adults often like to eat sunflower seeds as much as birds do. The children can also package the seeds with a homemade birdfeeder and give the gift to a friend or relative.

The chart on the facing page gives a list of plants suitable for a pet garden. If your pets differ from those in the list, head to the library or a veterinarian's office to do some research on the fresh food likes and dislikes of your pets. Then plant away!

Fall Holiday Garden

The fall holidays, Halloween and Thanksgiving in particular, are perfect for garden projects, thanks to the fall harvest. Pumpkins, gourds, ornamental corn, and popping corn all make their way onto our holiday tables, in some

Plant	Holiday	Comments
Pumpkins		
Jack-be-Little or Baby Boo	Halloween and Thanksgiving	Small pumpkins that make perfect table decorations.
New England pie	Thanksgiving	Makes rich holiday pies.
Tom Fox	Halloween	Perfect for jack-o'-lanterns.
Rocket	Halloween	The biggest pumpkin you'll ever grow—12 lb. to 20 lb. average. Great for jack-o'-lanterns.
Gourds		
Tuck's Turban	Halloween and Thanksgiving	Colorful scarlet squash with a striped button of silver, green, and white.
Shenot Crown of Thorns	Halloween and Thanksgiving	A unique, multicolored gourd with 10 fingers pointing toward the blossom end.
Dipper	Halloween and Thanksgiving	Can be made into a ladle.
Bottle or Birdhouse	Halloween and Thanksgiving	Can be used as a birdhouse or bottle.
Ornamental corn		
Little Jewels	Thanksgiving	Mini corn with purple husks and multicolored kernels.
Mandan Bride	Thanksgiving	Brilliant colored kernels.
Alamao-Navajo Blue	Thanksgiving	Traditional indian corn used for decoration and flour.

form, and can be incorporated into crafts to personalize the holidays (I'll talk more about garden projects in Chapter 8).

Your children can grow gourds of all shapes, colors, and sizes, as well as miniature pumpkins that *maybe* measure 3 in. across. Ever seen a white pumpkin? Well, they exist and are easy to grow, both in full and miniature sizes. The little ones, known as Baby Boo, are unique favors at a Halloween costume party.

With thoughts toward Thanksgiving, ornamental corn growing and drying in the garden is a beautiful site. You can

Butterflies will fascinate and delight your children. (Photo by Derek Fell.)

Gourds come in many varieties, all of which look lovely on a fall holiday table.

purchase seeds for red, blue, white, and variegated varieties of corn, all of which can be dried and displayed on front doors and holiday tables. (See the chart on p. 126 for a list of plants suitable for a fall holiday garden.)

A Flower Garden for Winged Visitors

Butterflies and hummingbirds are wonderful additions to a family garden. However, you will have to give some separate thought to attracting these winged visitors, as flowers—not vegetables—summon them to a garden.

Both butterflies and hummingbirds are attracted to sweetly fragrant flowers, and hummingbirds will only visit if such a flower—with sweet nectar for them to drink—is obvious and in full bloom.

To attract both of these beautiful creatures, encourage your children to plant a small flower garden near the

Plant	Attracts
Annuals	
Cosmos	Hummingbirds, butterflies
Fucshia	Hummingbirds
Heliotrope	Butterflies
Impatiens	Hummingbirds
Mignonette	Butterflies
Morning glories	Hummingbirds, butterflies
Nasturtiums	Hummingbirds
Scented geraniums	Hummingbirds
Snapdragons	Hummingbirds
Sweet alyssum	Hummingbirds, butterflies
Perennials	
Beebalm	Hummingbirds
Butterfly bush	Butterflies
Delphinium	Hummingbirds
Dianthus	Butterflies
Foxglove	Hummingbirds
Honeysuckle	Butterflies
Lavender	Butterflies
Lilac	Butterflies
Phlox	Hummingbirds
Salvia	Hummingbirds

vegetable plot or add some annuals to their existing flower garden. Be sure the children plant flowers in groups of several varieties or masses of a single variety and choose bright flowers of red, purple, yellow, orange, and white. (See the chart at left for a list of plants that will attract these two winged visitors.)

Butterflies are attracted to these flowers regardless of where they are planted. Hummingbirds, on the other hand, will prefer the bright flowers to be protected by margins of trees or shrub borders. They will also be more likely to stop by if they find nectar or sweetened water in a bird feeder.

Hummingbirds are attracted by flowers full of nectar and by sweetened water or nectar in a bird feeder. (Photo by Ken Druse.)

CHAPTER EIGHT

Family Garden Projects

There are many fun and interesting things you and your children can make from and for your family's garden. For this chapter I have chosen a variety of simple activities suitable for children of almost any age.

You and your children will learn how to make a scarecrow, a pressed-flower card, personalized pumpkins, garlic braids, cornhusk dolls, and an apple wreath. You will also learn how to save seeds from this year's garden so that you can grow the same plants next year.

Select just one project with your children. Begin carefully and slowly. Read the instructions, talk to your children about the final result, and divide up responsibilities. After the first project has been finished and the children see what they can build from some simple materials, they'll be clamoring for more.

Scarecrow

Farmers have been making scarecrows to keep birds away from their crops for more than 2,500 years. In ancient Greece, people made wooden statues of boys to scare birds away from their grape and wheat crops. In medieval England, farmers used live scarecrows, employing boys to stand in the middle of planted fields and flap their arms to

A scarecrow is just one of many garden crafts you and your children can make during the growing season.

A traditional scarecrow has a pumpkin head, but a bucket or an old basketball will work quite well, too.

scarecrows, the straw man from *The Wizard of Oz* (the materials list is on the facing page).

The straw man is the model against which most children and adults measure the perfection of their own scarecrows. But don't hold the children to perfection. Instead, let them be as creative as they'd like, adapting this plan to whatever suits them. There is nothing wrong, for instance, with a spaceman scarecrow, a grandma scarecrow with a flowing skirt, or even a poodle scarecrow.

Directions

Begin with the frame. Cut a 4-ft. crosspiece from a piece of 1x4. Then place the crosspiece about 2 ft. from the top of the 6-ft. main post and nail it in place with two 1¼-in. nails (roofing or drywall nails will work) to create a frame resembling a cross (see the drawing on the facing page). Make a point on the bottom of the main post so that it can be stuck into the earth when the scarecrow's completed.

Attach the head, trying to steady it as much as possible. If you use a pumpkin for the head, cut a hole just big enough to fit the top of the wood frame. If you use an old paint can or bucket, secure it to the crosspiece of the wood frame with wire or string. If you prefer a pillowcase head, stuff it and stick it onto the frame. Nestle the top of the main post into the stuffing. Then close the pillowcase at the bottom by tying string or wire around the main post.

Next, put a shirt on the crosspiece, using the wood on each side of the main post as arms. Button the shirt, tie

chase circling crows away from ripening wheat and barley. In early America, the Pilgrims made human-looking scarecrows at the suggestion of their Native American neighbors to keep the crows from depleting the corn crop. Today, scarecrows still appear in gardens and farms around the world, standing watch over the plantings.

A scarecrow is an enjoyable and useful craft for children to construct for the garden. Here I've given directions for a traditional scarecrow—one similar to the most famous of all

- One 10-ft. 1x4 for the frame
- Two 1¼-in. nails (roofing or drywall nails work well)
- Something for the head: a pumpkin, a pillowcase stuffed with newspaper, straw or packing paper, or a large paint can or plastic bucket
- Clothing for the body: an old shirt, pants, skirt, boots or shoes, jacket, whatever you and the children can find or spare
- Stuffing for the body: hay, straw, newspaper, old bed sheets, shredded packing paper
- String or wire
- Safety pins
- Accessories: hats, gloves, vests, suspenders, jewelry, anything you and the children can find to make a happening scarecrow
- Cornstalks and hay bales (optional as decorations)

the cuffs around the crosspiece with string, and tie the shirt waist around the main post. Then fill the shirt—sleeves and all—with stuffing, packing it in as full as possible.

Put pants on the scarecrow. Use the main post as one leg and let the other leg fall free. Fasten the pants to the shirt using safety pins and tie the pants at the ankles with string. Stuff the pants fully, then stick the pant legs into an old pair of boots or shoes.

Accessorize the scarecrow with a hat, jewelry, scarves—whatever you can find and spare. Now the scarecrow is ready to be placed in the garden. Come Halloween time, the children can position the scarecrow on the front steps of the house, garnished with hay bales and cornstalks.

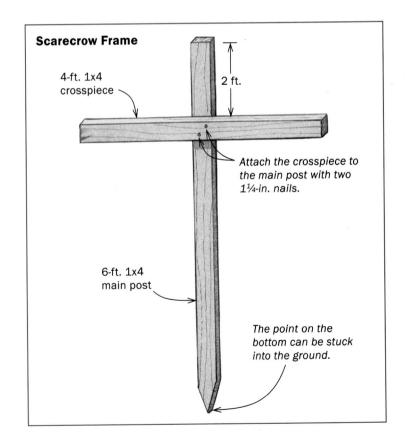

Scarecrow Frame

4-ft. 1x4 crosspiece

2 ft.

Attach the crosspiece to the main post with two 1¼-in. nails.

6-ft. 1x4 main post

The point on the bottom can be stuck into the ground.

Children will have fun designing and making cards with the flowers they've grown, dried, and pressed themselves.

Pressed-Flower Card

Pressed flowers can be used to make attractive note and greeting cards for any occasion and are particularly lovely when accompanying gifts from the garden. The cards can even be mounted in store-bought picture frames and displayed. These cards are particularly special to children when they contain blossoms of plants grown in an herb or vegetable garden.

This project will take some time to make, but the result will be a gift or memento of which your children will be very proud. I've provided directions here for making one card (the materials list is on the facing page). If your children plan on making more than one, adjust the materials accordingly.

Directions

Work with your children to select and clip some lovely, colorful specimens from your garden for pressing. After collecting the flowers, have the children brush off pollen, soil, or bugs with a small paint brush before pressing them.

To retain their color and delicate shape, flowers (and other plants) must be pressed when they are fresh and dry. Damp or wet plants will grow mold or turn mushy and dissolve into the blotting paper when they are pressed. If the plants wilt before pressing, place their stems in some cool water to perk them up. When they are refreshed, dry the stems.

Place a piece of blotting paper (available at craft and art-supply stores) on top of a square of corrugated cardboard. Then carefully lay out the

MATERIALS FOR A PRESSED-FLOWER CARD

- Fresh, dry flowers for pressing, picked by the stem (good choices are bachelor buttons, bleeding hearts, cosmos, daisies, Johnny-jump-ups, lavender, nasturtiums, pansies, and squash blossoms)
- Flower press
- Small scissors or utility knife
- Florist tape
- Tweezers

- Small paint brush
- Blotting paper (two pieces per pressing)
- 12-in. squares corrugated cardboard (two pieces per pressing)
- Rubber cement
- 8x11 sturdy, decorative paper
- Clear contact paper

plants on the paper, placing the petals, stems, and leaves in their preferred design. It may be necessary to tape down sturdy stems with florist tape (available at craft stores and florist shops) to hold them in place during pressing. Once the design is finished, place another piece of blotting paper on top of the flower, followed by another piece of cardboard. You can stack three or four flower pressings in this manner.

Next, place the stack in a flower press and tighten the bolts down firmly. (You can buy a flower press at craft and art-supply stores for about $10.) If you do not have a press, place one or several heavy books, such as dictionaries or reference books, on top of the stack. To keep the stack together, you may need to wrap tape, string, or a rubber band around it before setting the books on top. Place the drying flowers in a warm, dry place with good air circulation.

Within a week or two, each flower will dry and flatten in the very shape you designed when you laid it on the blotting paper. Be sure to handle the flowers very carefully, as they are quite delicate and can easily break or float away. Use tweezers to carry them, and keep them stored on pieces of cardboard in a notebook or box to prevent them from being damaged.

To make a pressed-flower card, choose some beautiful, decorative paper from an art-supply store, perhaps handmade paper with feathered edges. Fold the paper in the middle to form a card. Then affix the flower (or flowers) of your choice to the front of the card with a drop of rubber cement. You can also glue the flower to a piece of paper, then glue it to the card.

After affixing the flowers to the card, place a piece of clear contact paper over the front of the card. The contact paper will allow you to see the flowers while providing a protective layer for these delicate plants. Cut the contact paper to fit the front of the card and be very careful as you lay the sticky side down. Press out any air pockets with your fingers. You have to be gentle around the flowers, so use a cotton swab to press the contact paper down in areas close to the flowers.

Once the rubber cement and contact paper have dried, the card is ready to use. Along with their message, encourage the children to write a small description of the flowers in or on the back of the card. Whatever the card is used for and whoever it is sent to, the combination of the personal effort and the presentation of the delicate plant makes this craft a gracious gift. For added decoration, encircle the card's envelope with a thin, colorful, silk ribbon.

Personalized Pumpkins

There is nothing more fun for young children than searching the pumpkin patch in early fall and finding pumpkins growing with their names on them. The first time I tried this very easy project, I did it secretly for my then 3- and 10-year-old sons. Several weeks later, when it was time to pick the bright orange globes sitting in the back garden, I sent the boys out to see how many they could find.

A few joyful shrieks later and they were running to tell me about the magic that had happened in the garden: The pumpkins had "Seth" and "Bennett" labeled right into the rinds! Not only were my children's names on the pumpkins, but there were also Beth and Peter pumpkins (for mom and dad) and Oscar and Cyrus pumpkins (for the family's lovebird and poodle). The only question we were never quite able to answer was what a lovebird or poodle would do with a pumpkin. We made pies out of those.

Directions

Pumpkins have to be personalized when they are fairly young and green. So select a pumpkin that is either completely green or green with slight orange streaks just appearing. If the pumpkin is all orange, it's simply too late to personalize.

Once you and your children have selected the pumpkin, use a large nail, knitting needle, or cooking skewer to etch the name into the rind of the pumpkin. Use just enough pressure when etching to cut no more than $1/8$ in.

Etch your children's names into young, green pumpkins. By fall, the patch will be full of orange, personalized pumpkins.

into the rind. Any deeper than that, the pumpkin could rot or get infected.

Once the name has been etched into the pumpkin, turn it so that the part with the name on it is either facing the sky or getting a good flow of air around it. If the scratched surface should end up facing the ground, your chance of losing the pumpkin to rot, disease, or pests is quite high. As the pumpkin grows, the names that were etched in the rind essentially heal with a pale beige scab (there's a word the children will understand), while the rest of the pumpkin ripens to a deep orange.

Try expanding the pumpkin varieties you choose to personalize. For instance, tiny Jack-Be-Little pumpkins can be personalized and used for place settings at a Halloween party or at a

You and your children can personalize pumpkins in the garden using cooking skewers, nails, or even knitting needles.

Thanksgiving day gathering. Baby Boo mini pumpkins, which grow with a ghostly white skin, also personalize well and make terrific table or school decorations.

Even squash can be personalized in the same manner. Large blue hubbard squash, for example, can easily provide enough squash for a Thanksgiving

gathering of 10 to 20 people. This type of squash can be fun to personalize for a school class or scout troop and presented to a church food pantry or soup kitchen for the holiday meals these organizations sponsor.

Garlic Braids

Making a garlic braid is one of my favorite garden crafts. It is easy to do, useful to hang in your kitchen if you use a lot of garlic, and treasured as a gift. To make a garlic braid, you'll need a few garlic bulbs and some string or twine. If you'd like, you can decorate the braid with other useful items, such as dried red peppers or dried herbs, and present it as a wonderful holiday present. You and your children can also make a few braids to be sold as part of a fund-raiser for a children's organization or community charity.

Directions

Choose 10 or 12 garlic bulbs with tops that are still pliable and somewhat green, rather than brittle and stiff. It is important that the garlic bulbs you choose be of the softneck variety, which has stiff stems that resemble scallions. Stiffneck garlic has large cloves with sticklike stems that can't be braided.

For help in making the braid, follow the drawings on the facing page. First, trim the roots to a minimum of ½ in. and strip the outer wrappers and leaves from the stems and bulbs.

Lay three bulbs together on a work table with the stems facing you. Braid the stems two or three times until you have about a 1-in. braid with the

Garlic braids are fun fall projects and can be given to friends and relatives as holiday gifts.

Making a Garlic Braid

Step 1

Braid the stems of three bulbs two or three times until the braid is about 1 in. long.

Step 2

Place a fourth bulb on top of the braid. Hold its stem together with the last stem you crossed over. Treat these two as one. Make one or two more braids, ending with a single stem on top.

Step 3

Add a fifth bulb to the single stem on top. Continue as in step 2, ending with a single stem on top. Continue until all the bulbs have been braided together.

Step 4

Extend the braid 6 in. beyond the last bulb. Tie a piece of string around the braid to secure it. Then make a loop with another piece of string to hang the braid.

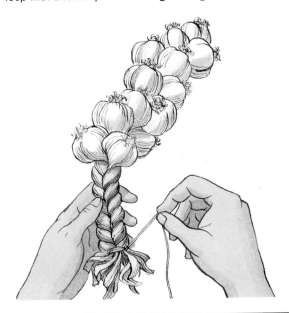

stems. Place a fourth bulb on top of the forming braid. Hold the fourth stem together with the last stem you crossed over. Make one or two more braids in these two stems, ending with a single stem on top.

Add a fifth stem and bulb to the single stem on top and continue braiding, ending once again with the single stem on top. Continue braiding in the same manner until you have braided all the bulbs together. The braid will form under the bulbs, and the number of stems you are braiding will vary as you add stems and bulbs.

Once you have added all of the garlic bulbs you want, continue braiding until the stems extend about 6 in. beyond the last bulb. Tie a string tightly around the braid to secure it. Trim the ends of the stems neatly and make a loop of the remaining string to use for hanging. (The same technique can be used to braid shallots or onions for a unique and edible kitchen decoration.)

Cornhusk Dolls

Cornhusk dolls are a traditional Early American garden craft, perfect as home decorations or holiday gifts. They are easy for children to make with very few, easily obtained materials (see the list on p. 140), even if your family chooses not to grow corn in the garden.

I typically have as much fun as the children when making cornhusk dolls, and it has become a yearly tradition in

Making cornhusk dolls is a wonderful, fun way for adults and children to spend a fall afternoon.

Making a Cornhusk Doll

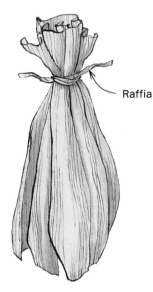

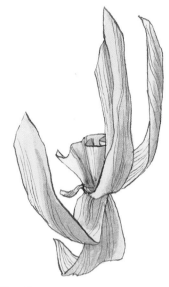

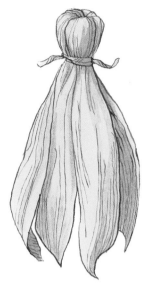

Raffia

Step 1
Gather four cornhusks and tie them at the narrow ends with raffia.

Step 2
Roll all the husks up over the tied portion.

Step 3
Tie the husks near the top with a piece of raffia. This will form the head and neck.

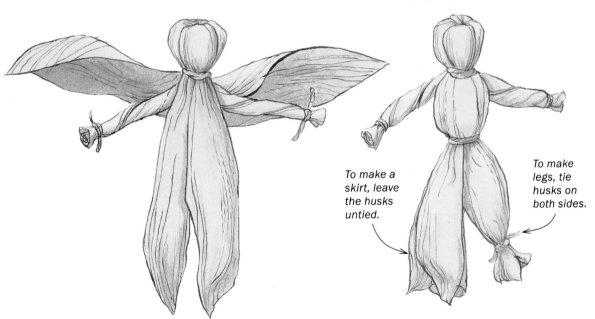

To make a skirt, leave the husks untied.

To make legs, tie husks on both sides.

Step 4
To form the arms, roll a long husk up to resemble a pencil. Tie the arms in the center and on the ends. Lift up the rear two husks and slip the arms underneath.

Step 5
Pull the rear husks back down over the arms and tie all the husks together at the waist with raffia. Make legs or a skirt, and the doll is ready to be accessorized.

MATERIALS FOR CORNHUSK DOLLS

- 12 to 15 cornhusks
- Large bowl of warm water
- Cotton cloth or paper towels
- Raffia
- Scissors
- Corn silk

my family. Last year my sons decided to make three wisemen dolls as Christmas-tree decorations. But before these dolls became the wisemen, they were cornhusk commandos, packing twig weapons and camouflaged with moss. Regardless of what type of dolls your children decide to make, you'll find them having fun and using their creative energy to the fullest.

Directions

If you plant a corn crop, save the husks (discard the tough outer layer) for this project. If you have not grown corn, use husks from a farmstand, store-purchased corn, or those packaged as tamale wrappers. Dry the husks on a cooling rack or on a piece of screening hung in a cool, dark, airy spot. The husks should dry in about a week.

When you are ready to make the dolls, put the dried husks in a large bowl of warm water and let them soak for about 15 minutes. The warm water makes the husks very pliable and easy to shape without breaking. Take the husks out of the water only as you need them, and leave the others to soak.

To make a doll, start with the body (see the drawings on p. 139 for help). Remove four husks from the bowl of water, dry them with a cotton cloth or paper towel, and stack them with all of the narrow ends together. About 1 in. or 2 in. from the narrow ends, tie the husks together with a piece of raffia.

Holding the bundle between your thumb and forefinger, turn it so that the short end of the tied husks is on the bottom. Separate the husks and, one by one, pull them down over the raffia, holding each husk with your thumb as you roll it over and down. You should pull the husks down as smoothly as you can without tearing them.

Spread the husks around evenly and tie them with a piece of raffia to form the neck and head.

To form the arms, roll a long husk up to make it look like a pencil and tie it in the center and at both ends with raffia. Position the body so that the smoothest side of the head is facing you and lift the two top husks away from the others that make up the doll's body. Push the arm against the tied neck, under the two lifted husks, and fold these husks back down over the arms. Smooth the two husks down against the body of the doll and tie them to the body just below the arms to form the waist.

Position the arms while they are still damp. My young friend Whitney tied the arms of her doll together with raffia and then made a tiny baby bundle to set in the doll's arms.

If you want a female doll, leave the bottom husks spread out to form a skirt. If you want a boy doll, tie the husks together with raffia to form legs.

There are many ways to accessorize the doll. For instance, wrap another husk around the doll's head or shoulders to make a shawl. Then tie this at the waist with raffia, making a bow in back of the doll. You can also wrap a large, perfect husk around the waist, over the ends of the shawl to make an apron. Tie this in the back to hold just the apron or both the shawl and the apron. Large, loopy bows will look quite delicate running down the back of the doll.

To add color to the doll, try dyeing some cornhusks with food coloring and using these colored husks for the shawl and aprons or other accessories. You can also use colored corn silk to make hair for the doll.

When the work is done, trim the skirts, aprons, or legs so that the doll can stand on its own. Cornhusk dolls traditionally have no faces, but there is no reason why you and your children could not add some features to the face. (Use pencil because ink will spread throughout the husk.)

There are many ways to customize cornhusk dolls. Add a scarf, a hat, a shawl, or even a baby in its mother's arms.

Apple Wreath

I first made a wreath from an old coat hanger and dried apple slices a few years ago when my apple tree had borne too much fruit and I had no more room for (nor more interest in making) applesauce. The construction was rustic, but the effect was charming. I garnished the wreath with a colorful ribbon and gave it to my best friend's

An apple wreath can adorn a kitchen, bathroom, or bedroom, bringing a touch of the outdoors into your home.

daughter, Emma, for Christmas. The wreath was greeted with such acclaim by Emma that I decided to make a wreath or two each fall, sometimes keeping them and sometimes giving them away.

Apple wreaths are perfect for kitchens, bathrooms, and bedrooms. You can even make tiny wreaths using lady apples. These tiny wreaths make wonderful Christmas-tree decorations.

The size of the wreath, the apple color, and the decorations are up to you (see the materials list below for a traditional apple wreath). I have used cinnamon sticks, whole nutmegs, pinecones, and dried flowers to decorate the wreaths, as well as just about every kind of ribbon you can imagine. Gather the children and have them stretch their imaginations to design a wreath. Whatever type they make, the wreath is sure to have a particular charm that will give the children a sense of pride.

MATERIALS FOR AN APPLE WREATH

- About 18 medium-size apples, either golden or red delicious
- 4-qt. bowl of cool water
- 1 teaspoon lemon juice
- Paper towels or cotton cloth
- Yarn or embroidery thread
- Darning or embroidery needle
- One thin wire coat hanger, white or brown in color
- Colored ribbons

Directions

Work with your children to collect about 18 firm, medium-size apples—perfect in color, skin, and shape. Gather apples that are uniform in size and balanced in shape, with the fruit evenly distributed around the center core of the apple. Lopsided apples make lopsided wreaths.

Cut the apples horizontally into ⅛-in.-thick slices (if your children are too young to use a sharp knife, do this yourself). Do not peel or core them, as the peel provides the color, and the core allows the apples to withstand being suspended from the coat hanger. (My family typically discards the smaller slices from the bottom of the apple, but you can use these to make tiny wreaths.)

Fill a 4-qt. bowl with cool water and add a teaspoon of lemon juice. Drop the apple slices into the bowl of water. After 8 to 10 minutes of soaking, remove the slices and pat them dry with a paper towel or cotton cloth. I often spread the slices out on newspaper covered with paper towels and blanket the apple slices with another piece of paper towel so that both sides of the slices dry well.

Once the water has been absorbed, thread these slices on a long piece of thread or yarn fitted with a darning or embroidery needle. Hang the apples in a well-ventilated place. Stretch the thread out across a doorway, for instance, and separate the slices so that no two are touching.

The apple slices are dry enough for wreath making when they feel like

Pick your favorite-color apples and slice them uniformly to help guarantee a lovely wreath.

leather (this could take as long as three weeks, depending on the heat and humidity levels). Remove the apples from the thread and spread them carefully out on a table for inspection. Encourage the children to examine the slices carefully and throw away any that have been bruised in the drying process. Then, make the frame for the wreath.

Help the children untwist the hook part of a wire coat hanger and stretch out the wire until it is as straight as possible. This will require some bending and rebending of the wire to remove the angles formed when the lower part of the hanger was made. Do

Bend a coat hanger into a round frame, then carefully slide the dried apple slices on it, being sure not to damage the slices.

not, however, lose the shape of the hook part of the hanger, which will act as the hanger for the wreath. Shape the wire into a circle and smooth it repeatedly until you have a fairly smooth and even circle. Since the apple slices will hide the actual wire and mask any small inconsistencies in the shape, do not worry if your circle is not perfect.

Work with the children to slip the apple slices onto the wire. Thread the wire through the hole in the apple core. Place as many slices on the wire as you can, pushing them together gently so that the wire is not visible when you look at the wreath. Help the children retwist the hook back together. Use

colored ribbon to decorate the wreath at the base of the hook. If you want to cover the bare wire on the hook, put rubber cement on it and wrap it with ribbon.

To add scent to a wreath, add cinnamon sticks or fresh anise stars or nutmegs. To maintain the sweet smell, you may have to rub these items with an emery board every once in a while. The scents will last a few days after that.

Saving Seeds for Next Year's Garden

At the end of the season, you and your children will have just completed quite a gardening adventure. You will have planted, watered, weeded, and harvested your way through nearly six months of learning, exercise, and fun. To duplicate the success of this year's garden and to help make next year's garden even better, have the children save seeds from the garden, so they can plant some of their favorite crops next year.

Along with producing the same terrific crops, there are three other benefits to saving seeds. First, you will save money because you won't have to buy a lot of new seeds. Second, you will have seeds for plants that you know thrive in your climate. For instance, you may live in an area that requires plants to adapt to particular conditions, such as little water or extreme temperatures. If you find a fruit or vegetable variety that does well in your geographic area, saving the seeds will ensure that you

Planting seeds from last year's garden will allow you and the children to grow some of your favorite fruits and vegetables this year.

can continue to grow and experiment with that variety. Third, vegetable plants and seeds slowly change their genetic makeup. Indeed, you may not be able to purchase a seed one year from your favorite purveyor that you purchased from that same dealer the year before. Saving seeds will provide you with a yearly supply of your favorite plant seeds.

Be aware, though, that hybrids sometimes revert to one parent, not the hybrid form. So if you save seeds from a hybrid plant, you may not get the same plant the following season.

The keys to saving seeds successfully are to choose seeds from healthy plants, then dry and store them appropriately.

Choosing healthy seeds

To decide which plant seeds to select, look at the whole plant and consider the following characteristics.

• Color: Select seeds from plants with healthy, vibrant color. Deep green leaves without blemishes are often signs of healthy, vigorous plants. Also, save seeds from plants that produce colors that are unique and beautiful to the eye but might not be available from your favorite farmer's market every season, such as golden cherry tomatoes or red and white tomatoes.

• Earliness: Save seeds from plants that produce fruits or vegetables earlier than others, particularly if you have a short growing season.

• Drought resistance: Plants that require little water or that can weather spells of dry weather may be particularly valuable, depending on where you live and on the availability of water.

• Disease resistance: Many of us cannot avoid disease, no matter how hard we work to keep our garden free of problems. Choose seeds from plants that hold up under certain diseases and still produce a healthy harvest.

• Hardiness: One problem northern gardeners often face is wanting to produce plants that often can't weather the cool nights of late summer and early fall. Save seeds from those plants that hold up under changing weather conditions, including high winds, arid heat, and chilly nights.

• Insect resistance: Some plants will still produce wonderful fruit even when their leaves are ravaged by beetles or mites. These plants have developed a resistance to those insects, so try to save these seeds for future plantings.

• Lateness to bolt: Many early spring plants, such as lettuce and spinach, grow beautifully until the first true warm weather appears. When the warm weather sticks around, these plants tend to bolt (or go to seed) quickly and will turn bitter. Look for early spring plants that can still grow in the heat without bolting quickly. These plants will help

you extend your harvest well into the first several weeks of summer.

• Uniformity: There's no more wonderful sight to a gardener than several plants of the same variety producing fruits or vegetables uniform in looks and taste. If you have grown 10 tomato seedlings that each produce large, juicy, and sweet fruit, the plant has uniform qualities that are worth saving.

• Vigor: Examine the plants from top to root. If they look healthy and hardy, grow well throughout the season, with large amounts of high-quality produce, you have vigorous plants worth reproducing next season.

• Flavor: Save seeds from the plants that taste the best. If your children will only eat one kind of cherry tomato, save these seeds to ensure a similar crop next year.

• Productivity: Some plants produce more fruit than others. Save seeds from the most prolific producers.

• Shape: Many children will not eat fruit with bumps, ridges, dips, and scars. Save seeds that produce fruits or vegetables that have pleasing shapes.

• Storage ability: Some plants can be stored more effectively than others, such as potatoes, carrots, and squash. Save seeds from plants that store better for the winter.

Scooping seeds out of mature fruits and vegetables for saving is messy, but that's the fun part for the children.

Drying seeds

Before storing them, seeds must be dried, since moisture will rot the seeds and render them useless. For some plants, collecting and drying the seeds are pretty simple.

To save seeds taken from pods, for instance (beans and peas), you must first let the pods dry completely. Then, to break the seeds free, thresh the pods by rubbing or beating them. Once the seeds have been removed from the pods, place them on a screen to dry a bit further. Once they have dried on a screen with some good airflow for a week, they are ready for storage.

Not all seeds are as easy to retrieve and dry, however. To gather seeds that form inside a fruit or vegetable (tomatoes, summer squash, and cucumbers, for instance), the work is a bit more complicated but will be well worth it. (The project is a great learning lab for budding scientists, as well.)

Choose mature fruits or vegetables, so the seeds will be fully formed. For some plants, such as summer squash or cucumbers, this means letting them grow bigger than you normally would. Then simply cut open the fruit or vegetable and scoop out the seeds.

Some plants, such as tomatoes and cucumbers, need the seeds to be fermented to remove gelatinous sacks around the seeds and to destroy diseases. To do this, place the seeds in a small bowl, with either a bit of water or preferably juice from the plant, and cover with plastic wrap. Place the bowl in a warm spot until the fermenting gases make the plastic bulge and the seed mixture bubble.

Retrieve the seeds from the bowl, wash them in a clean bowl of water, stirring vigorously. Pour off any debris and hollow seeds that float to the top, then pour the rest through a strainer. (Make sure the seeds can't pass through the strainer!) Rinse the seeds in the strainer under running water.

Wipe the bottom of the strainer with a towel and dump the seeds onto a glass, metal, or ceramic sheet. Do not dry the seeds on paper or cloth because the seeds will stick to these materials. Place the sheet with the seeds in a warm, dry area, but not in direct sun. Temperatures over 96°F can destroy the seeds, so have the children track the temperature carefully. Most seeds will be dry enough for storage in about a week.

Storing seeds

As I said before, moisture will rot saved seeds, so once they have been thoroughly dried, store the seeds in a moisture-proof, airtight container. Glass jars with rubber seals, metal containers with moisture-proof seals, or locking freezer bags work well. (Do

Glass canning jars with metal lids and bands are perfect for saving seeds.

The following organizations will help you contact other gardeners who save seeds. Through these organizations, you'll be able to get a lot of seed-saving information, as well as leads to getting some wonderful, hard-to-find heirloom varieties.

Native Seeds/SEARCH
2509 N. Campbell #325
Tucson, AZ 85719

Seed Savers Exchange and
The Flower and Herb Exchange
Route 3, Box 239
Decorah, IA 52101
$1 for information

not use lightweight sandwich bags, as they will allow moisture to get inside.)

Store the seeds in a freezer or refrigerator, or in a very cool place, such as a basement or cellar as close to the floor as possible (remember, heat rises). Be sure to label the containers so you know which container holds which seeds. And make sure the labels stick. One fall, my family saved lots of squash, pumpkin, and gourd seeds, but the labels fell off the containers while they were in the basement. The following spring we were not exactly sure what seeds were in the containers.

Record information on your saved seeds in a garden journal. Note the type of plant, variety name, and name and address of the source (if you bought them or if they were given to you). Write down the date obtained and the date the seeds were stored.

Once you and your children have your chosen seeds stored and

information on them recorded, consider starting a seed-saving club in their school or in your community. This type of club can be the perfect foundation for a pen-pal relationship with another school or community. By swapping seeds with children from other areas, your children will learn about different cultures, traditions, geographic conditions, and foods. They will also have the opportunity to grow plants that no one else in their area may have ever heard of.

There are a couple of organizations that can put you in touch with other seed-saving gardeners, with particular emphasis on heirloom varieties (see the sidebar above). Contact one of these groups for more information on seed saving, as well as for some truly wonderful and unique seeds.

USDA Plant Hardiness Zone Map

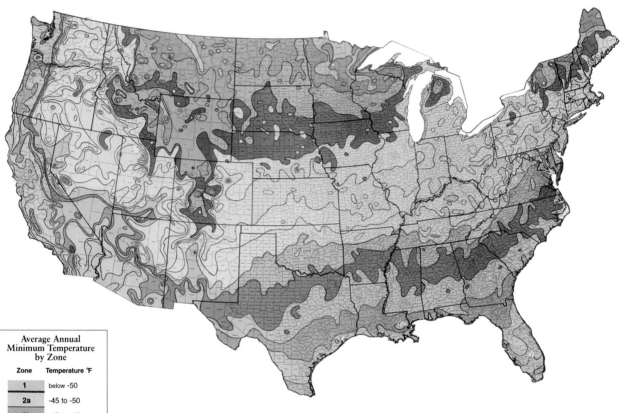

Average Annual Minimum Temperature by Zone	
Zone	**Temperature °F**
1	below -50
2a	-45 to -50
2b	-40 to -45
3a	-35 to -40
3b	-30 to -35
4a	-25 to -30
4b	-20 to -25
5a	-15 to -20
5b	-10 to -15
6a	-5 to -10
6b	0 to -5
7a	5 to 0
7b	10 to 5
8a	15 to 10
8b	20 to 15
9a	25 to 20
9b	30 to 25
10a	35 to 30
10b	40 to 35
11	40 and above

This map shows the United States divided into 11 zones. To use the map, simply find the zone where you live and choose plants designated to grow well in your zone. Be aware, however, that other factors, including soil, exposure, moisture, and drainage, affect the growth of plants.

Resources

Sources for seeds

Here are some mail-order seed catalogs that I recommend because they are well-annotated, well-depicted, and filled with unique plants.

Bountiful Gardens
18001 Shafer Ranch Rd.
Willits, CA 95490
(707) 459-6410
Catalog, free.

Burpee
300 Park Ave.
Warminster, PA 18974
(215) 674-8233
www.burpee.com
Catalog, free.

The Cooks Garden
P.O. Box 5010
Hodges, SC 29653-5010
www.cooksgarden.com
(802) 824-3400
Catalog, free.

Johnny's Selected Seeds
Foss Hill Rd.
Albion, ME 04910
(207) 437-4301
Catalog, free.

Le Jardin du Gourmet
Box 75F
St. Johnsbury Center, VT 05863
(802) 748-1446
Catalog, $1.

Peaceful Valley Farm Supply
P.O. Box 2209
Grass Valley, CA 95945
(530) 272-4769
Catalog, free.

Sandy Mash Herb Nursery
316 Surrett Cove Rd.
Leicester, NC 28748-5517
(704) 683-2014
Catalog, $4.

Seeds of Change
P.O. Box 15700
Santa Fe, NM 87506-5700
(505) 438-8080
Catalog, free.

Select Seeds
180 Stickney Hill Rd.
Union, CT 06076
(860) 684-9310
Catalog, free.

Shepherd's Garden Seeds
30 Irene St.
Torrington, CT 06790
(860) 482-3638
Catalog, free.

**Southern Exposure
Seed Exchange**
P.O. Box 170
Earlysville, VA 22936
www.southernexposure.com
(804) 973-4703
Catalog, $2.

Vermont Sunflower Farm
P.O. Box 455
Johnson, VT 05656-0455
(802) 635-2253
Catalog, free.

Vesey Seeds, Ltd.
P.O. Box 9000
Calais, ME 04619
(902) 368-7333
Catalog, free.

White Flower Farm
P.O. Box 50
Litchfield, CT 06759-0050
www.whiteflowerfarm.com
(800) 503-9624
Catalog, free.

Wolf Mountain Farms
HC6 Box 137
Doniphan, MO 63935
(573) 255-3650
Catalog, free.

Useful websites for gardeners

Garden Escape
www.garden.com
A free interactive, innovative, and informative site for home gardeners. You can ask gardening questions and find help in designing your own garden. You can also buy seeds, plants, and tools.

Garden Net
www.trine.com/GardenNet/
Provides free interesting gardening information and unique on-line services. You can search for garden catalogs, check out over 600 gardens across the U.S., and find many links to other garden-related websites.

Plant Adviser
www.plantadviser.com
A free service designed to help you make informed decisions about the plants you buy and grow. Here you can search for plants that thrive in particular climate regions, with lots of photos of plants. The service focuses on plants that are available in most retail nurseries and garden centers.

Real Gardeners
pages.prodigy.com/
Real.Gardeners/
Free service provided by nonexperts of the garden world—just regular folks who enjoy gardening. Here you can find gardening tips, ask questions, and tour gardens around the world.

Index

A

Airflow, importance of, 24
Amendments, efficient use of, 34-35
Apple wreaths:
  making, 143-44
  materials for, 142
Arsenic, in treated wood, 40

B

Beams, cutting, 41
Black plastic:
  benefits of, 81
  conserving water with, 84
  as mulch, 81
  placing, 81
  planting through, 81
Boron, as plant nutrient, 50
Broccoli:
  days to maturity of, 17
  pest problems with, 17
Butterflies, attracting, 127-28

C

C/N ratio, defined, 53
Calcium:
  deficiency of, 50
  as plant nutrient, 50
Carbon:
  materials, high, 53
  and nitrogen, 53
  See also C/N ratio.
Carrots:
  Baby, 14
  Early Chantenay, 14
  Imperator, days to maturity
    of, 13
  maintaining bed of, 13
  Nantes, days to maturity of, 13
  quick-maturing, 13-14
Celery:
  days to maturity of, 16
  extending growing season of, 16
  growing, 16
Cell flats:
  number of seeds in, 67
  See also Containers, for starting
    seeds.
Children, measuring arms of, 38
Climate, and plant choices, 7
Cold frames, hardening off seedlings
    in, 75, 78
Collars, as pest barriers, 98
Compass points, locating in yard, 25
Compost:
  adding, to beds, 60-61
  benefits of, 52
  bin for,
    building, 55, 56-57
    buying, 54
    locating, 24
  and children, 52
  collecting organic matter for,
    53-54
  creating, 52-55, 57-60
  materials to avoid, 54
  organisms in, 53
  pH of, 52

pile,
  C/N ratio in, ideal, 53
  moisture in, 57
  size of, 55, 57
  turning, 55
science of, 53
screening, 58
smell of, 58
sources of, 59
tumbler, 54
when ready, 58
  See also Composter.
Composter:
  building, 56-57
  materials for, 56
  See also Compost.
Containers, for starting seeds:
  adding growing medium to, 67
  choosing, 66
  making, with newspaper, 66
  old, reusing, 66
  rotating, 70
Cooperative Extension Service, for
    soil testing, 48-49
Copper, as plant nutrient, 50
Corn:
  locating, 28
  sweet,
    days to maturity of, 16
    harvesting, 16
    planting, 16
    starter for, 16
Cornhusk dolls:
  making, 140-41
  materials for, 140
Cotyledons, defined, 71
Crops:
  cool-weather, 102-104
  cover, winter, 106
  interplanting, 102-103, 104
  long-season, 104
  short-season, 104
  successive planting schedule for,
    103
  warm-weather, 102-104
Cucumbers:
  Oriental, days to maturity of, 13
  pickling, days to maturity of, 13
  quick-maturing, 12-13
  slicing, 12
    days to maturity of, 13

D

Direct seeding:
  tools for, 72
  when required, 72
Double digging:
  benefits of, 59
  explained, 59-60

F

Fall holiday garden, plants for,
    126-27
Family meeting:
  to assign responsibilities, 19
  to choose plants, 8
  at end of season, 31

Fencing, as pest barrier, 98
Fertilizer tea, defined, 62
Fertilizers:
  chemical, disadvantages of, 61
  cost of, 45
  efficient use of, 34-35
  organic,
    applying, 62
    types of, 61
    when required, 60-61
Flower garden, plants for, 127, 128
Flowers, pressing, 132-33
  See also Pressed-flower cards.

G

Garden detectives, becoming, 92-93
Gardening:
  child-sized tools for, 20
  finding time for, 19
  organic,
    approach to, 42-45
    importance of, 44-45
    key to, 45
    rules for, 45
Gardens:
  allies in, 90, 92
    list of, 92
  assigning duties for, 19-20
  building, 37-41
  circular, laying out, 115
  cleaning, 106
  cleanliness of, 97
  drawing plans for, 26, 28-30
  enemies of, 92
  journal for, 110
  locating, 23-25
  locations of, harmful, 25
  maintaining, 19, 20, 83
    See also Pruning. Thinning.
      Watering. Weeding.
  maximizing space in, 21
  purpose of, 21
  sizing, 18-21
  themes for. See Fall holiday gar-
    den. Flower garden.
    Heritage garden. Pasta
    garden. Pet garden.
    Pizza garden. Snack
    garden.
  watering, 84-87
  well-sited, example of, 24
  See also Plans. Raised beds. Row
    gardens.
Garlic, planting, in fall, 107
Garlic braids:
  making, 136, 138
  materials for, 136
Grow mats, for warming seedlings,
    69
Growing medium, soilless:
  benefits of, 64
  contents of, 64
  for starting seeds, 64
  working with, 64
Growing season, extending, 101-105

H

Hardening off, of seedlings:
  benefits of, 74
  in cold frames, 75, 78
  defined, 74
  schedule for, 75, 79
Hardiness zones:
  defined, 7
  identifying, 7
Harvesting:
  methods of, 105
  timing of, 105
Heritage garden:
  Mexican,
    plants for, 122
    recipes for, 123
    researching, 122
  researching, 120-22
Home soil test kit, accuracy of, 48
Hornworms, controlling, 94
Hummingbirds, attracting, 127-28

I

Insects:
  catchers for, 94
  identifying, 94
Iron, as plant nutrient, 50

L

Lettuce:
  days to maturity of, 17
  harvesting, 17
  locating, 28
Lighting, for seedlings:
  fluorescent, 69
    placement of, 70
  grow, 70
    placement of, 70
  sunlight, 69

M

Magnesium, as plant nutrient, 50
Manganese, as plant nutrient, 50
Master gardeners, advice from, 43
Melons:
  days to maturity of, 17
  growing, 17
  locating, 28
  trellising, 17
Molybdenum, as plant nutrient, 50
Mulch. See Black plastic.

N

N-P-K ratio:
  balanced, achieving, 61
  defined, 50
The New Victory Garden (Thompson,
    Bob), mentioned, 71
Newspaper, making pots with, 66
Nitrogen:
  and carbon, 53
  excess of, 50
  levels, increasing, 50
  materials, high, 53
  See also C/N ratio. N-P-K ratio.

O

Organic pest management (OPM), discussed, 91
Overwatering, indications of, 87

P

Parsnips:
  harvesting, 107
  planting, 107
Pasta, sauces for, 116
Pasta garden:
  plants for, 116, 117
  recipes for, 118
Paths:
  wide, in raised beds, 34
  width of, 38
Peas:
  locating, 28
  sugar snap,
    days to maturity of, 17
    harvesting, 17
Peppers, locating, 28
Pesticides, cost of, 45
Pests:
  animal, preventing, 96
  eliminating, 93
  identifying, 92
  infestation of, symptoms of, 95
  management of, organic, 91
  preventing, 97-100
Pet garden:
  as gift source, 125
  plants for, 124, 125
pH level:
  balancing, 51
  defined, 50
  optimum, 50
  testing for, 50
  See also Soil: acid level of; alkaline level of.
Phosphorus:
  benefits of, 50
  deficiency of, 50
  levels, increasing, 50
  See also N-P-K ratio.
Pizza:
  picking toppings for, 114-15
  recipe for, 113
Pizza garden:
  plants for, 111
  recipes for, 113
  shape of, 115
  tomato sauce from, 112
Plans, for gardens:
  felt,
    making, 27
    materials for, 27
  changes in, 31
  displaying, 31
  drawing, 26, 28-30
  filling in plant data boxes on, 31
  locating plants on, 28
  materials for, 26
  scale for, 26, 28
  tracking changes on, 31
Plant data boxes:
  defined, 30
  filling in, 31
Plant data sheets:
  making, 22-23
  as reference for drawing plans, 30
  sample of, 22
Plant food. See Plants, nutrients for.
Plant lists:
  making, 6, 8-12
  See also Plants.

Planting areas, well-defined, for children, 33
Planting:
  in rows, 72-73
  schedule of, successive, 103
  through black plastic, 81
Plants:
  choosing, 6, 8
  and climate, 7
  companion,
    defined, 99
    list of, 98
  cool-loving, 28
  deep-rooting, 104
  family favorites, 8
    expanding, 11-12
  for family garden, 12-17
  handling, 74
  hardiness zones for, 7
  health of, and cleanliness, 97
  heat-loving, 28
  nutrients for, balance of, 50
  quick-maturing, 9
  shallow-rooting, 104
  spacing requirements of, 21
  See also Crops. Plant data sheets.
    Plant lists. Seedlings.
    Specific plants.
Pot bound, defined, 77
Potassium:
  benefits of, 50
  deficiency of, 50
  levels, increasing, 50
  See also N-P-K ratio.
Potatoes, days to maturity of, 17
Pots:
  making, with newspaper, 66
  See also Containers.
Pressed-flower cards:
  making, 132-34
  materials for, 133
Pruning:
  benefits of, 101
  when necessary, 101
Pumpkins, personalized:
  making, 134-36
  materials for, 134

R

Raised beds:
  accessibility of, for children, 37
  advantages of, 33-36
  appropriateness of, for plants, 36
  edging material for, 38-40
    See also Wood, for raised-bed frames.
  framing for, 40-41
  height for, 38
  paths in, 37-38
  planting areas in, 33-34, 35-36
  sizing, 37-38
  soil temperature of, 35
  use of amendments in, 34-35
  use of fertilizers in, 34-35
  width for, 38
  working soil in, 34-35
Row covers, floating:
  as pest barriers, 98
  purpose of, 82
  using, 82
Row gardens:
  planting areas in, 35
  soil temperature of, 35
  use of amendments in, 34
  use of fertilizers in, 34

S

Scale, of garden plan, 26
Scarecrows:
  frame for, 131
  history of, 129-30
  making, 130-31
  materials for, 131
  types of, 130
Seaweed, as fertilizer, 62
Seed catalogs:
  choosing, 7
  climate-specific, 7
  for plant information, 22
  as reference, 8-10
Seedlings:
  the best, choosing, 77
  buying, 76-77
  examining, 99
  feeding, 74
  handling, 74
  hardening off, 74-75, 78-79
  lighting amount required, 74
  planting, 74, 80, 82
  pot-bound, 77
  protecting, 82
  separating, 71, 74
  transplanting,
    to garden, 79-80, 82
    to larger pots, 74
    tools for, 79
  watering, 82
Seeds:
  drying, 147
  newly planted,
    germinating temperature of, 68
    lighting requirements of, 69
    watering, 68
  planting, outdoors, 73
  removing, from plants, 147
  saving,
    benefits of, 144-45
    choosing for, 145-46
    organizations for, 149
  sowing depth of, 67
    clay-coated, 67
  spacing of, in containers, 67
  starting,
    fun methods of, 65
    indoors, 64, 66-71, 74, 75, 78, 79
  storing, 148-49
Snack garden:
  plants for, 119
  recipes for, 120
Soil:
  acid level of, 50-51
    decreasing, 51
    excess of, 50-51
  alkaline level of, 51
    decreasing, 51
    excess of, 51
  amending, 106
  amendments for, organic, 52
    See also Compost.
  basics of, for children, 45-52
  chemical composition of, 48-52
  clay-type,
    benefits of, 47
    characteristics of, 47
    loosening, 47-48
  contaminants in, 51-52
  loam-type,
    amending, 48
    characteristics of, 48
  nutrient levels in, 49-50

peat-type,
  amending, 48
  characteristics of, 48
pH level of, 50-51
preparing, 52-55, 57-62
samples of, taking, 49
sandy-type,
  amending, 48
  characteristics of, 48
structure of, 47
temperature of,
  in raised beds, 35
  in row gardens, 36
testing, 48-49
types of, 47
when to work, 46
See also Double digging.
Space, efficient use of, 34
Spinach, locating, 28
Sulfur, as plant nutrient, 50
Sunlight:
  importance of, 24-25
  maximum amount of, for seedlings, 69
  minimum amount of, 25

T

Thinning:
  benefits of, 100
  when necessary, 101
Thompson, Bob (The New Victory Garden), mentioned, 71
Tomatoes:
  days to maturity of,
    beefsteak, 15
    berry, 14
    miniature, 15
    plum, 15
  locating, 28
  quick-maturing, 14
Tools:
  child-size, 78
  for children, 20
  cleaning, 49, 97
  for transplanting seedlings, 79
Traps, as pest barriers, 98

W

Warming, of newly planted seeds, 68-69
Water, conservation of, 84, 85
Watering:
  bottom-, 68
  ease of, 24
  frequency of, 86
  methods of, 68, 85, 86
  of newly planted seeds, 68
  schedule for, 20, 69
Weeding:
  fun methods of, for children, 89
  importance of, 87-88
Weeds:
  harmful effects of, 87
  identifying, 88
  preventing, 89
Winter rye grass, as cover crop, 106
Wood, for raised-bed frames:
  cedar, 40
  cutting, 41
  redwood, 40
  treated, 40

Z

Zinc, as plant nutrient, 50

Book publisher: Jim Childs

Associate publisher: Helen Albert

Editorial assistant: Cherilyn DeVries

Editor: Thomas McKenna

Designer: Ken Swain

Layout artist: Lynne Phillips

Illustrator: Scott Bricher

Photographer (except where noted): Lynn Karlin

Typeface: Minion

Paper: 80-lb. Utopia Two Gloss

Printer: Quebecor Printing/Hawkins, Church Hill, Tennessee